T0116496

SOCIAL MEDIA MUSINGS

Book 5

GEORGE WAAS

authorHOUSE®

AuthorHouse™
1663 Liberty Drive
Bloomington, IN 47403
www.authorhouse.com
Phone: 833-262-8899

Published by AuthorHouse 03/07/2023

ISBN: 979-8-8230-0279-0 (sc)
ISBN: 979-8-8230-0278-3 (e)

Library of Congress Control Number: 2023904091

Print information available on the last page.

Any people depicted in stock imagery provided by Getty Images are models, and such images are being used for illustrative purposes only. Certain stock imagery © Getty Images.

This book is printed on acid-free paper.

CONTENTS

Introduction..xi

Arizona Senator Leaves Democratic Party. No
Surprise Here 1
Religious Freedom Or Discrimination? 3
Which Republican Party Do You Belong To? 6
Florida Is The Freest State In America—Nonsense
From Florda's Governor DeSantis................................... 7
A Sad Commentary On Our Times 9
There's A Price To Be Paid.... 10
Is Trump Too Big To Prosecute? 14
To Indict Or Not To Indict, That Is The Question.......... 19
Equal Justice Under Law 20
Who Are The Great Conservative Thinkers Being
Denied Access To Our Colleges And Universities? 23
It Can't Happen Here, Can It? 25
Why Do Extreme Right Wing Republicans Support
Putin? 26
DeSantis' Latest Effort At Attacking Science And
Appealing To His Crowd In The Run-Up To 2024 26
Mitch McConnell Is Looking For A Few Quality
Senate Candidates 31
"Not Guilty By Reason Of Insanity." 36
This Is Not The Christmas Spirit; This Is A Cruel
And Heartless Act 39
Unhinged And Deranged. And Not Worth The Effort... 41
Honored Conservatives Or A Rogues' Gallery? 44
Immigration: A Philosophical Divide With
Migrants As Pawns 45

Republican Party Leaders Remain Silent In The
Face Of This Latest Embarrassment 48
Let Them Help Re-Elect Joe Biden 51
Bits And Pieces: 54
House Republicans Are In Search Of A Speaker
While Donors Are Concerned With The Party
Looking "Stupid." 59
Some Thoughts On Fact Vs. Belief 60
New Year's Resolutons And Bucket Lists 64
How Important Is One's Reputation? 69
What Does The Score Of House Republicans
Really Want? 73
Two Years Ago: There Is Still Darkness 77
The Danger Of Sanctimoniousness 81
The Goal Of The Republican Party Is To Destroy
Liberalism Of The 1930s And Beyond, And
Replace It With Right-Wing Ideology 84
The Path Forward: Darkness Or Enlightenment? 90
The January 6 Committee Report 96
Toward A Theocratic Judiciary 100
There Is Blood In The Water; Time For The Sharks
To Attack 102
Take Your Soma; You'll Feel Better, Be Distracted,
And Won't Ask Annoying Questions 106
Joe Biden, Government Records, And Chain Of
Custody 110
Lies, Fraud, Hypocrisy, And The Constitution 112
Nixon. Reagan. Clinton. Trump. Biden. It's Not
The Crime; It's The Cover Up 116
A Delicate Balance 120

More Revelations Of Records Found On Joe
Biden's Property: He Needs To Stop The Bleeding 124
The Filibuster: A History 125
Some Republicans Believe Today's Republican
Party Is The Party Of Lincoln. They're Wrong 130
Should Police Be Immunized From Lawsuits? 135
Newspaper Editorials Are Essential In A Free Society... 140
Journalism May Be Dead, Just Not In A Way
Readily Understood..................................... 144
The Sad State Of American Print Journalism–And
A Personal Story 147
A Note On Appropriation Of Funds And Their Use.... 152
Have Conservatives Been On The Right Side Of
History? When? 154
Conservatives And Liberals: A Comparison.............. 156
Plant A Tree, Have A Child, Write A Book—That's
Immortality 159
The Value Of Pets In Our Lives.........................163
Presidential Leadership............................... 168
Indoctrinaton And Brainwashing. What's The
Difference? 175
Bette Davis Was Right: "Getting Old Isn't For
Sissies." 178
Judicial Interpretation Of The Constitution 183
Art Does Imitate Life................................... 186
House Oversight And Fairness? Hardly..................... 190
A Primer On Government Records, Classified Or Not... 195
For The Republican Whatabouters........................... 198
The Republican Party's Moment Of Truth Is Fast
Approaching..202

"Ignorance Is Bliss" 205

A Sobering Thought... 209

The Latest To Practice The Art Of Deflection And
Delay: Mike Pence 216

There Is Nothing Wrong With Teaching Theories
As Theories. This Is Done Every Day 218

Pence Has A Rough Road Ahead In Trying To
Avoid A DOJ Subpoena For His Testimony On
January 6 221

Partial Georgia Grand Jury Report Full Of Sound
And Fury, Yet Signifies Nothing................................. 226

A Sad Commentary On The Right Wing's Most
Loyal Audience 227

Republicans Could Learn A Few Lessons 232

Is Trump Helping Himself By Blasting DeSantis? 236

DeSantis Is Now An Expert On International Affairs . 242

Social Security And Medicare Are Safe For Now,
But Eternal Vigilance Is Necessary 246

What Are Republicans Drinking?................................ 249

"A Basket Of Deplorables"... 253

What Will Political Leadership Look Like Ten
Years From Now?... 258

Kevin McCarthy Has Sold His Soul To The
Extreme Right Wing Of His Party. Here's A Clear
Example 264

"Shameless" 267

Another Comment About A Proposed Law That Is
Destructive Of Florida Education 275

"True Colors" 278

Sacrificing Wisdom For Gratification 282

On IQ Tests, America Ranks 29Th In The World;
Florida Ranks 38Th Among The States. Is This
Significant In Measuring Intelligence As It Relates
To Political Preferences? 288
RNC Chair Says Presidential Candidates Must
Sign A Loyalty Pledge To Take Part In 2024
Debates. Dream On 292
The Republican Party Is The Party Of Law And
Order? Think Again 294
What Is Your Story Worth? 299
Who Is Really Engaging In "Cancel Culture?" 304
Fox News Repeated The "Big Lie" To Protect Its
Brand And Preserve The Conservative Point Of
View. Deplorable 307
After Putting Disney In Its Place, Gov. Ron
DeSantis Takes Aim At The Press By Proposing A
Change To Defamation Law 309
"Don't Worry Be Happy" 311

INTRODUCTION

In 2022, I wrote a book titled "Social Media Musings." In the introduction, I said I am the product of two professions driven by inquiry and skepticism, journalism, and law.

I noted that both professions are founded upon logic, rational thinking, critical analysis, and sound judgment. So, when I see something that doesn't make sense, defies logic, is irrational, or otherwise off-the-wall, I ask questions and search for answers.

I also confessed that I am a Facebook junkie, although not necessarily enamored with social media. There is certainly far too much misinformation, flat-out wrong information, etc., being spread on social media. And we know that "a lie travels around the globe while the truth is putting on its shoes."

In that book, I said that, for the most part, I kept my opinions to myself, or shared them with family and friends, until the January 6, 2021, attack on our nation's capital. Since then, taking to heart the note on the Facebook page that says, "What's on your mind," I've posted my thoughts and opinions about various situations on a variety of subjects. Many of my posts are quite lengthy, solely because of the importance I place on fact, analysis, reason, logic, critical thinking, and sound judgment.

I then included in my book, in chronological order from January 6, 2021, to February 2022, my posts on a variety of subjects, mostly—but certainly not all— on politics. Since that book was published in March 2022, I continued to post of Facebook, hoping to continue a national dialog on issues of great public importance, which resulted in Book 2, which was also published in 2022. But I didn't stop there. I also published Book 3 that same year. But I didn't stop there. I published Book 4 a few months later. This is my fifth and final book on this subject. I will continue posting on Facebook; I won't include those posts in future publications—unless I change my mind.

I hope that by this time, it is obvious that social commentary makes up the overarching theme of my posts. The purpose of social commentary is to provide discussion, including analysis, on social, cultural, political, or economic issues that affect all of us. A major theme of social commentary is to implement or promote change by informing the general public about a given problem and appealing to people's sense of justice.

And from what we've experienced over the past few years, we need change.

You don't have to be a famous entertainer or athlete to engage in social commentary. All too often, we equate fame and notoriety with intelligence and depth of thought. Having a social conscience doesn't depend on fame or notoriety; in fact, there are some whose opinions are influential solely because of fame or recognition; the reality is they haven't a clue what they're talking about. Further, as the 2022 election campaigns played out, there were several candidates who repeatedly demonstrated ignorance and stupidity, yet garnered millions of votes. Ignorance and stupidity must never become fashionable or acceptable. Enlightenment must always trump darkness.

What allows a person to offer meaningful social commentary is being sufficiently educated to comment rationally and reasonably on relationships among people and between people and their government.

At the heart of any social commentary lies an agreeable set of facts. Without agreement on observable, tangible facts, discourse and commentary become virtually impossible. It is toward that end that these musings are primarily directed.

Here is Book 5 of my social media musings on Facebook.

ARIZONA SENATOR LEAVES DEMOCRATIC PARTY. NO SURPRISE HERE

Ariz. Sen. Kyrsten Sinema's decision to leave the Democratic Party is a surprise to no one. She's been unhappy as a Democrat, and with her colleague Sen. Joe Manchin, has been a thorn in the side of the Senate Democrats for the past two years.

Pointedly, she didn't opt to join the Republican Party. Smart move, since both her fellow senator, Mark Kelly, and newly elected governor, Katie Hobbs, are Democrats.

This gives her time before she must run again in 2024 to decide which way the wind is blowing. She doesn't like the so-called "tax-and-spend" liberals, but I doubt she wants to run into the arms of a political party whose leader dines with bigots and anti-Semites, and who favors trashing parts of the Constitution that he says prevented him from being elected. And Republican election denier and Trump loyalist Kari Lake just found out that being both isn't a sure way to get elected governor of Arizona.

The Democrats did far better in this past election cycle than expected. The Republicans did poorly, judging from expectations going in to that election period.

Going forward, we can expect to see continued unfavorable press for Trump and the Republican Party. There are those criminal cases, and the public mood seems to be souring on Trump's incessant wailings about his poor treatment, lack of appreciation, and overall victimization mentality. Yet, the mood of the country is still sour, so she can float between both parties and pick and choose those things she will support and those she won't.

This gives her freedom and flexibility; but it doesn't prevent her from having to choose down the road.

Meanwhile, while Democrat policy initiatives will largely be stalled or watered down in the House, the Senate will for the most part give Biden his appointments and whatever else he can get without the House's involvement. And you can bet the mortgage there will be few, if any, judicial vacancies by the end of 2024.

So, Sen. Sinema must consider carefully her choices going forward. After all, Arizona is not exactly a red state. If the Republican Party doesn't shed itself of its current baggage, she may have no option but to run as a Democrat. That certainly didn't hurt Kelly or Hobbs this year.

The Republicans will no doubt make a big push for her to join Mitch McConnell, Ted Cruz, Lindsey Graham and their merry gang of right wing rabble rousers. However, if she's smart, she'll want to foster a reputation as a maverick and ultimately go with the choice that most assures her re-election. Still, it would be wise for her to remember the old adage: be careful what you wish for.

RELIGIOUS FREEDOM OR DISCRIMINATION?

What happened here was inevitable backlash.

Four years ago, the Supreme Court ruled in favor of a Colorado baker who refused to bake a cake to celebrate the marriage of a same sex couple because of his religious objection. The Court expressed respect for those with religious objections to gay marriage, but also noted: "Our society has come to the recognition that gay persons and gay couples cannot be treated as social outcasts or as inferior in dignity and worth."

Flash forward to last week, when a restaurant in Richmond, Virginia canceled a reservation for a group of Christians whose members have the same religious beliefs and objections as this Colorado baker.

The USA Today columnist contends that the restaurant's act is sheer bigotry while the group's beliefs are in line with valid religious teachings and therefore can't be considered discriminatory. She also notes that another Colorado baker continues to refuse to create specialty cakes for same-sex weddings and gender transitions based on his religious beliefs.

A few days after the restaurant cancelled the Christian group's reservation, the Supreme Court's conservative majority appeared sympathetic to a website designer who didn't want to be forced to design sites for same-sex weddings because of her religious beliefs about marriage.

The columnist takes the restaurant to task for being intolerant to the religious beliefs of this group. To her, there is a vast difference between the freedom from compelled acts against one's religious beliefs, and a business's decision not to provide a basic service. The former is perfectly fine; the latter is unvarnished bigotry. In essence, the argument here is the difference between ordering someone to create something that goes against religious beliefs on one hand, as opposed to simply providing a basic service like serving a meal on the other. It is self-evident that if one act can be protected by religious freedom, then it's easy to dismiss any notion that the act is bigotry. To this columnist, the issue is black and white.

But let's flip the coin here to show how oversimplified is this columnist's treatment of this issue.

It's not a quantum leap for the restaurant's management and staff to contend it's against their religious, moral and constitutional beliefs to discriminate against LGBTQ+ community members, and that they can't be forced to serve those who frown upon their status and regard them as, in the words of the Supreme Court decision of four years ago, "social outcasts or as inferior in dignity and worth."

Can you see what's coming to the Supreme Court down the road here? Recall the phrase "what's good for the goose is good for the gander."

Looking at this through the restaurant's eyes, when staff prepare the food--cooked a certain way--place it on the plate in a certain way, served by wait staff dressed in fancy garb, etc., there is a certain amount of creative expression involved here, and this is just as much an act of expressive liberty as designing a cake or website. I'm not referring to hash houses or fast food joints here. If you've been to fancy, upscale restaurants, you know exactly what I'm referring to. You are certainly familiar with restaurants that tailor their menus to a customer's particular taste.

The management and staff could well view the religious claim by a cake or website designer as a cover for bigotry, regardless of the Court's take on this issue.

There are lots and lots of fancy, top of the line restaurants out there whose ownership and management echo the sentiments of this Virginia restaurant. You can bet there's a lawyer out there (probably lots of them) who's already working on crafting a constitutional argument that by cooking that chateaubriand to the customer's taste; arranging it on a designer plate with perhaps a little flower; and creating that special dessert with chocolate, strawberries and whipped cream; each employee is in essence engaging in a work of expressive creativity protected by the First Amendment; and further, it's against their religious beliefs to discriminate against anyone regardless of reason.

It would not be a difficult to argue that the creative effort involved by the restaurant is no less expressive than creating a design for a single cake or a single website that can be used for multiple customers. All that would be needed is the creation of a single template.

But that case is for another day.

WHICH REPUBLICAN PARTY DO YOU BELONG TO?

I happened to be scrolling down my Facebook page when I came across a post noting 27 celebrities who support the Republican Party. This gave me pause, because the question that occurred to me is which Republican Party?

There are two.

The first adheres to the principles of traditional conservatism: limited government, less taxes, free market capitalism, deregulation of corporations, individual accountability, etc. Reps. Liz Cheney and Adam Kinzinger are two most prominent because they bucked the House Republican leadership by serving on the House January 6 investigating committee. There are others, but they are becoming fewer and fewer.

The second is forged by Donald Trump and dutifully followed by his loyalists and supporters; their beliefs include the Big Lie of a rigged election, election denying, stoking violence to stop a constitutional electoral process, promoting baseless and outrageous conspiracy theories, endorsing or siding up to bigots and anti-Semites, etc.

As you can readily see, there is a world of difference between the two versions of the Republican Party. Traditional conservatives express their differences with Democrats over policy choices. The fringe right wing differ with Democrats and moderate Republicans over the very nature of our form of government.

When someone professes to be a Republican, it's fair game to ask which Republican Party he/she actually belongs to.

FLORIDA IS THE FREEST STATE IN AMERICA— NONSENSE FROM FLORDA'S GOVERNOR DESANTIS

During the recent Florida trial over the potential reinstatement of Democratic State Attorney Andrew Warren, whom Gov. Ron DeSantis suspended after Warren signed a pledge not to prosecute abortion seekers or providers, attorneys for Warren asked DeSantis' aides to define "woke."

Taryn Fenske, DeSantis' Communications Director said "woke" was a "slang term for activism…progressive activism" and a general belief in systemic injustices in the country.

Asked what "woke" means more generally, DeSantis' General Counsel Ryan Newman, representing DeSantis, said "it would be the belief there are systemic injustices in American society and the need to address them."

Newman added that DeSantis doesn't believe there are systemic injustices in America.

A poll conducted earlier this year by UMASS Amherst Poll found that over half of Americans believe white people in America have advantages based on skin color; 75% believe public schools should teach about racial inequality.

But because DeSantis' belief system refuses to recognize what a majority of Americans believe, he is right and there is no room for dissent. He must bend those who disagree to his will by punishing them. Hence, his war on wokeness.

Because in his words, Florida is where the belief in systemic injustices and the need to fix them go to die. If conditions cause discomfort or unease, simply say they don't exist; and those who dare to point them out are to be disciplined, removed from office, and punished until they, like the governor, put their heads in the sand and pretend what is real doesn't exist.

This, in a nutshell, is what he means when he says Florida is the freest state in America.

A SAD COMMENTARY ON OUR TIMES

The other day, I saw a Facebook post that I found both sobering and sad. The subject was the upcoming holidays, and that people of varying faiths who will be visiting their places of worship in celebration and remembrance. The message was for those attending to be alert and use caution. The message is certainly a sobering one, considering the frequency of attacks on people who are considered "different" from the attackers.

But what saddened me is the number of posts that said if only Donald Trump had been allowed to finish his wall at the nation's southern border, none of these problems would exist. That's the key: in their mindset, it's these illegal aliens who are causing all these problems.

Sadly, this is categorically untrue. The nation's national security apparatus has made it abundantly clear that the most serious threat to our national security is right wing domestic violence: the kind we saw marching in Charlottesville, Va.; attack our nation's Capital on January 6; threaten the lives of the Speaker of the House, the former Vice President, Michigan's governor and others who dare challenge them; and those who utter baseless claims about Blacks, Jewish people, the gay community, and just about anyone else who's different.

We need more better angels to come forth and deal with fact, not opinion based on fear.

THERE'S A PRICE TO BE PAID....

"No man is above the law and no man is below it: nor do we ask any man's permission when we ask him to obey it." Theodore Roosevelt.

Ours is a "government of laws and not of men." John Adams.

These words have guided our nation from its inception to the present.

The Rule of Law, not the rule of kings, is a founding principle of our country. It remains a core principle that defines who we are as Americans.

The Constitution is supreme; no one pledges an oath to any individual. Article VI. Section 3 is clear on this matter:

"Senators and Representatives, and the Members of the several State Legislatures, and all executive and judicial Officers, both of the United States and of the several States, shall be bound by Oath or Affirmation, to support this Constitution."

Whether these words, and others that serve as the bedrock upon which our Democracy is founded, will remain the nation's rule and guide will be vigorously tested over the next several months.

Politicians pride themselves on personal responsibility; that is, the willingness to both accept the importance of standards that society establishes for individual behavior and to make strenuous personal efforts to live by those standards.

Personal responsibility is important because no one else is responsible for accepting the consequences that follow one's actions and reactions. Personal responsibility is a crucial skill for living a successful life. It's a sign that each person take ownership of every aspect of his or her life, and each one is prepared to handle anything that comes his or her way.

Whether personal responsibility applies to all lawbreakers— including those officials impressed with the public trust-- will also be severely tested by those who sadly believe the law applies to others, not themselves.

Due to the thorough and diligent work of the House committee investigating January 6, we now know the extent of criminal charges the nine members unanimously recommends be brought by the Justice Department against former President Donald Trump and a host of his acolytes and henchmen, some of whom are elected public officials duty bound to obey the Constitution. Their utter failure to comply with the Constitution, federal law and the rule of law, will now be up to federal prosecutors and our federal judicial system.

There isn't a writer of political thrillers who could come up with the reality of what we've witnessed from Trump and his cronies over the past two-plus years. Yet, make no mistake about it; we are where we are because one man decided to take the law unto himself by lying about the results of an election, obstructing the orderly constitutional process of certifying that election, and resorting to violence in order to stay in power illegally.

Specifically, the House committee referred four major criminal charges against Trump to the Justice Department: obstructing an official proceeding, defrauding the United States, making false statements and giving aid or comfort to an insurrection.

Criminal charges against a former president is unprecedented; but so was the presidency and post-presidency of Donald Trump. These four charges are extremely serious and carry substantial maximum penalties.

In addition, what must not be overlooked is Trump's theft of government records—including highly classified documents—and his mishandling of these records at his Mar-a-Lago estate.

Then there are those cases in New York and Georgia—and who knows where else.

Yes, Trump certainly has a lot on his plate going forward into next year. None of it bodes well for him.

Of course, his henchmen and cronies are already going through their host of defenses: "fake news," "hoax," "witch hunt;" etc., anything that might deflect from the obvious: a tome of testimony and evidence, largely from Republicans including many in the Trump White House, that paints a damning picture of a president unleashed, venting anger and resentment against anyone who dared to challenge him.

The MAGAites won't read the report; it's very taxing to read something so lengthy and detailed, containing so much Republican testimony, and so damning of their hero. They'll just attach one or more of their dismissive labels to it, and that will make them happy. The rest, however, will be informed and, therefore, know better.

Even his VP foot soldier, Mike Pence, who showed some fortitude in not kowtowing to Trump's demand to decide the election for him, has now resorted to showing his wet noodle for a spine by saying he hopes Trump isn't indicted for his many crimes. He probably is saying that to appeal to the party base—which isn't going to vote for him anyway. Pence has become quite a pathetic figure, to say the least.

Trump has a lot to be held accountable for. He, as well as those who aided and assisted him in his many nefarious deeds, must now pay the price for their despicable conduct.

His behavior is now where it belongs, in the hands of prosecutors and the judicial system.

IS TRUMP TOO BIG TO PROSECUTE?

The cases against Donald Trump are not factually complex. This is not like an IRS tax case or corporate mismanagement litigation involving tens of thousands of documents laid out in a broad, convoluted mosaic requiring the best legal minds to unravel.

The facts supporting the four charges referred to the Justice Department by the House January 6 committee are relatively straightforward, graphically supported by riveting public testimony, videos and photos that gripped the nation though several televised public hearings over the summer, concluding yesterday.

Similarly, there is nothing in Trump's theft of government records, and subsequent mishandling of them, at his Mar-a-Lago estate that requires lengthy fact investigation. Trump's defense—that he can declassify records simply by thinking about it—while good for a laugh, also shows that all that is left for prosecutors on this matter is to take what he did and apply it to the law which clearly prohibits theft and mishandling of government confidential records.

If the House committee summary portends what's in the final, massive report, it will be as clear a path as possible to matching Trump's demonstrated conduct with the cited laws that he broke.

So, why is it taking so long for prosecutors to reach their decision when the facts and relevant law are relatively clear and straightforward?

One reason: the person facing criminal prosecution is a former president of the United States. Be assured that if this were only a John Doe, or even a sitting senator, governor or member of Congress, charges would have been filed some time ago.

The holdup (no pun intended) here is that, for the first time in American history, someone elected to the highest office in the land faces being treated as a criminal defendant.

Remember no man is above the law? Well, that sounds fine, except for those tasked with making the ultimate decision to prosecute must apply that to someone who, for four years, had the constitutional duty to "take care that the laws be faithfully executed."

Lawyers and judges are steeped in precedent. When handling a case, lawyers look to prior cases where the facts were similar or at least persuasive enough to argue their points. Judges look to prior cases to guide them in reaching their decisions and issuing their judgments.

The problem for prosecutors and judges here is that there is no precedent for charging a former president with crimes, and prosecuting him before a jury of his peers.

Note that last phrase: of his peers. Who are the peers of a former president? You can bet the mortgage that, should Trump be charged, his lawyers will argue that his peers aren't ordinary citizens whose names appear on the voting rolls. Rather, his peers are public officials (past and present) and his supporters, most notably cronies and MAGAites.

If this sounds ludicrous, remember it was Trump's lawyers who had no difficulty making ludicrous arguments following the 2020 election and going forward. Ludicrous will be no barrier for Trump's legal team. Outrageous is also not part of their vocabulary.

The point here is that Trump's lawyers will use every strategy, gimmick, ploy, etc., to challenge every word, syllable, character or letter uttered by the prosecution.

Briefly summarized, the four charges are as follows:

Trump obstructed an official proceeding of Congress with his repeated efforts to delay or deny the counting of the electoral votes on January 6 that would finalize the transfer of power to then-President-elect Joe Biden.

Trump committed a "conspiracy to defraud the United States," particularly when he offered to make Jeffrey Clark acting attorney general if Clark agreed to help him push the fake electors scheme by falsely claiming the Justice Department had found evidence of widespread voter fraud.

The committee also wrote that Trump entered into a "conspiracy to make a false statement" when he "conspired with others to submit fake electors to Congress and the National Archives."

And for the fourth criminal referral, they wrote that Trump sought to incite, assist or aid and comfort an insurrection. "President Trump was directly responsible for summoning what became a violent mob to Washington, D.C., urging them to march to the Capitol, and then further provoking that already violent and lawless crowd with his 2:24 p.m. tweet about the vice president."

On the first charge, ultimately, the certification process was completed, although delayed by the riot. On the second charge, Trump relented when several top Justice officials threatened to resign in masse if Clark were appointed. Trump's lawyers could argue that since these two worked out fine, there was no crime committed. Recall that proof of a crime requires intent; if Trump doesn't testify (and you can be certain he won't), the prosecution must still prove that he intended to commit a crime.

Of the four charges, the fourth is the most profound. Still, a president does have First Amendment rights, and whether his words actually directly led to the storming of the capital will lie at the heart of the prosecution and defense on this point.

Prosecutors must not only be fully prepared to meet an onslaught of defense strategies, but must also consider two other vital matters: first, the burden of proof in criminal cases is proof beyond a reasonable doubt; second, a jury verdict must be unanimous. You can bet Trump's lawyers will be focusing laser-like attention to creating doubt in the mind of at least one juror. And if they can get a MAGA on the jury, so much the better for Trump.

Thus, while the facts themselves aren't particularly difficult to parse, the status of the prime criminal defendant, coupled with the need for a unanimous jury and the need to overcome reasonable doubt, and the historical nature of the prosecution itself, make for a most daunting undertaking.

While two years is a relatively long time, it is also a target clock that Trump wants to run out. He knows that if he, or a right wing faithful, is elected in 2024, all criminal cases against Trump will be dropped. And those January 6 felons will get their pardons (or at least have hope that they will.)

The conflict prosecutors face is unprecedented. Faithfulness to the rule of law and that no man is above the law vs. the criminal actions taken by a president of the United States. The ultimate question is whether a president is simply too big to ever face criminal prosecution. I doubt our Founding Fathers would answer that question negatively.

We must keep the faith.

TO INDICT OR NOT TO INDICT, THAT IS THE QUESTION

Taking a line from William Shakespeare, the question now asked following the House January 6 committee's referral of four violations of federal law to the Justice Department is whether Donald Trump should or shouldn't be indicted.

For the first time in our nation's almost 250-year history, an elected head of state faces prosecution, trial and imprisonment for crimes committed while in office.

It's not easy to wrap one's head around this, for there is nothing that compares. America came close with Richard Nixon and his Watergate crimes 50 years ago, but his successor, Gerald Ford, pardoned Nixon and removed any prospect of criminal charges against a former president. Historians concluded that this single act cost Ford his election as president in 1976. Recall that Ford was appointed vice president by Nixon when Spiro Agnew resigned in disgrace.

Unlike Nixon's situation, should Trump be indicted, he will have no friend in the White House to issue a pardon.

Ultimately, the decision to prosecute lies with the Department of Justice. The appointed special counsel, lawyers and staff up to and including the attorney general will make the call.

The decision not to indict will send a seismic jolt across our nation's institutions; it will be the greatest stain on our judicial system. It will mean power matters. Money matters. Influence matters. Politics matter. And fear of Trump and Trumpism matter.

Profound questions will be raised over the historic arch that, in America, justice is blind, as represented by the scales of justice. In the words of William Penn, "Justice is justly represented blind, because she sees no difference in the parties concerned. She has but one scale and weight, for rich and poor, great and small."

We have long prided ourselves in believing that the law favors no one. America's justice system is premised on the notion that rich and poor, weak and powerful, are treated equally.

At least, that's the promise. We know all too well how the rich and powerful benefit by having resources not available to the poor or the weak. But this doesn't prevent our better angels from striving to be faithful to the proposition engraved on the West Pediment, above the front entrance of the United States Supreme Court building in Washington, D.C.:

EQUAL JUSTICE UNDER LAW

This means that the government and its leaders must also obey the law. Our Constitution was written in 1787. The writers of the Constitution wanted a government that was ruled by laws, not by men.

That is precisely what is at stake should Trump not be held accountable for his conduct.

Our history teaches that the law is supreme; each official takes an oath to the Constitution, not to any man. If a man is favored over the commands of the Constitution, the question will be asked whether we are truly a nation of laws or men.

The House January 6 committee spent more than 18 months amassing a voluminous tome of testimony and evidence that points to multiple criminal acts by Trump. That committee was faithful to its charge that a substantive investigation be done on behalf of the American people who believe in a judicial system that is blind to status and open equally to all. The public wanted the facts of what happened leading up to and including January 6. The committee gave them that in exacting gut-wrenching detail.

We will soon find out not only the depth of Trump's aberrant conduct, but why he fought so hard to prevent his tax returns from reaching the eyes of the public.

These bedrock principles of American justice will take a shattering, jolting hit if Trump is excused from accountability regardless of the severity of his offenses solely because of the office he once held.

Our entire system of government is predicated on faith; faith that the principles upon which our nation was founded are good, decent and worth preserving. If people lose faith in our institutions, we can't survive as a nation. This is most assuredly what is at stake here.

It isn't lost on anyone who's aware that the public image of the Supreme Court as the ultimate pillar of justice is in decline as a result of some recent ideological opinions at distinct variance with substantial public opinion. It isn't a leap of logic to conclude that further and perhaps more substantial erosion of faith in our judicial system will result if Trump is given a pass.

If Trump is indicted, we will find out whether his and his loyalists' threats of violence are real or just smoke and mirrors. Those who made these threats will have to ask themselves whether Trump is worth the risk to themselves and the country. There are already hundreds wallowing in jails in several states serving time for their January 6 insurrection involvement who are asking themselves whether what they did was worth it, since Trump remains free, living in luxury, and raking in millions off his con games.

If he's indicted, the litigation will be intense and of long duration, but the principles of American justice will have prevailed. The faith of our forefathers in our institutions will be strengthened.

Equal justice under the law will be honored. There won't be a double standard; an indictment will be faithful to the principle that the rich and poor, weak and powerful receive equal treatment under the law. Government leaders will again be held to obey the law. Power, money, influence and politics won't matter.

History tells us that senators, members of Congress, cabinet members, judges, as well as governors, other state and local officials have all been convicted of crimes and sentenced to jail time. But never a president.

That time is now upon us.

We must never become a nation where one man is too big to jail.

WHO ARE THE GREAT CONSERVATIVE THINKERS BEING DENIED ACCESS TO OUR COLLEGES AND UNIVERSITIES?

The other day, I read an article in which a leading Republican describes the extremes of both parties to a T. He said liberals are extreme over progressive issues, while the conservatives are extreme over insane rhetoric.

Then I read where conservatives believe their viewpoints are being frozen out of universities and colleges by liberal professors and administrators.

These two points got me thinking about what conservative viewpoints are being barred from college life. And who exactly are these informed, intelligent, articulate conservatives being barred from our institutions of higher learning?

We're most familiar with the usual description of conservativism: less government, less taxes, personal responsibility, etc. (Of course, whether the party faithful adheres to these self-professed bedrock principles is quite another matter. Making it against the law to discuss certain subjects or say certain words is certainly not an example of limited government; it is more an example of authoritarian central government thought control. Providing permanent tax cuts for the wealthy is certainly less taxes for them; this, however, doesn't help the working class or poor; nor does it help to fund programs for a majority of Americans. And avoiding subpoenas and fighting accountability for crimes are not examples of personal responsibility. But I digress.)

When conservatives complain about not having equal access to present their viewpoints, they usually are silent as to who precisely represents their philosophy.

Since they haven't provided a list of their greatest spokespersons, I will provide a list and ask conservatives to identify those who speak the same language as they do. Who represents true conservativism? And whether they agree with the statements made by these key speakers.

For starters, how about Donald Trump? Does he represent true conservative thought? How about Kevin McCarthy, who most likely will become House speaker after he sells his soul to the far right? Jim Jordan? Marjorie Taylor

Greene, Lauren Boebert? What about Ted Cruz or Lindsey Graham? Josh Hawley? Greg Abbott or Ron DeSantis? How about Kanye West, Nick Fuentes, Herschel Walker? Alex Jones? The leaders of the Oath Keepers and Proud Boys? Please feel free to add any name or names of your choosing.

And pray tell let us know what pearls of wisdom makes each selected spokesperson so faithful to true conservative thought.

IT CAN'T HAPPEN HERE, CAN IT?

The Taliban has suspended university education for Afghan women. Republican officials in America, in the name of freedom, crack down on what can be taught and what can't be said on college and university campuses.

But there is no relationship between the two here, right? There is no similarity between the repression in this faraway country and what is happening to academic freedom here, is there? Totally irrelevant situations, right?

There was no repression of speech, press and academic freedom during World War II, was there? The former Soviet Union and China never engaged in repression of speech, press and thought, did they? And Russia and China don't repress and punish transgressors today, right? Dictators and despots don't repress speech and press, do they? Dictators and despots fully support academic freedom, don't they?

"Those that fail to learn from history are doomed to repeat it." Winston Churchill.

WHY DO EXTREME RIGHT WING REPUBLICANS SUPPORT PUTIN?

Why do so many extreme right wing Republicans support Vladimir Putin in his war against Ukraine? Marjorie Taylor Green, Matt Gaetz, Paul Gosar and others have railed against providing aid to Ukraine. One noted extremist, Nick Fuentes, the Holocaust denier and known bigot who recently dined with Donald Trump, is on record as saying he wishes "Putin were president of America."

Whether Russia is in fact a purely socialist or communist country today, the image of Russia as a looming threat from the post-World War II cold war period of 1947-1991 still carries much of the day in America.

I thought Republicans vigorously oppose communism, socialism and dictatorships in all forms. Obviously, not all do.

DESANTIS' LATEST EFFORT AT ATTACKING SCIENCE AND APPEALING TO HIS CROWD IN THE RUN-UP TO 2024

On December 13, Florida Governor Ron DeSantis asked the Florida Supreme Court to impanel a statewide grand jury to "investigate criminal or wrongful activity in Florida relating to the development, promotion, and distribution of vaccines purported to prevent COVID-19 infection, symptoms, and transmission."

Specifically, DeSantis told the Supreme Court: "Florida law prohibits fraudulent practices, including the dissemination of false or misleading advertisements of a drug and the use of any representation or suggestion in any advertisement relating to a drug that an application of a drug is effective when it is not. The pharmaceutical industry has a notorious history of misleading the public for financial gain. Questions have been raised regarding the veracity of the representations made by the pharmaceutical manufacturers of COVID-19 vaccines, particularly with respect to transmission, prevention, efficacy, and safety. An investigation is warranted to determine whether the pharmaceutical industry has engaged in fraudulent practices."

Nine days later, five justices, three of them DeSantis appointees, approved the grand jury request.

No one should be in any way surprised by this.

This is a classic example of the logical fallacy known as poisoning the well—an attempt to commit a preemptive personal abusive attack against an opponent before that opponent has a chance to defend itself. DeSantis has already condemned the COVID vaccine companies—a favorite attack by vaccine deniers--now all he needs from his appointed doctors/vaccine deniers and pliant grand jurors overseen by a cooperative authority is something—anything—that he claims will support his indictment. No doubt his "investigators" will find something that will make DeSantis look good to those who buy into his charades as he moves forward toward his run for president.

Without offering a scintilla of evidence to the Court, DeSantis has already concluded that pharmaceutical companies have "a notorious history of misleading the public (and) questions have been raised (by vax deniers) regarding the veracity of the representations by the pharmaceutical manufacturers of COVID-19 vaccines…" Therefore, the governor concludes, "An investigation is warranted to determine whether the pharmaceutical industry has engaged in fraudulent practices."

More than 1.1 million Americans have died from COVID-19, including more than 83,000 Floridians. The American Medical Association and the vast majority of medical professionals say vaccines remain safe and effective at slowing the spread of COVID-19. We are by no means out of the woods on COVID. China is experiencing another explosion; we can only wonder if it spreads here again how the public will react after being fed what the governor is offering.

There is nothing in the governor's petition asking the grand jury to investigate the state's rollout of its strategy in dealing with this deadly disease; the number of deaths impacted by the rollout; or anything that even remotely suggests inquiry into the government's response, other than to oppose any mandatory mass vaccination program. How many deaths and illnesses could have been prevented by a more efficient, earlier rollout? This is not a matter for this grand jury. No surprise here.

It should not be lost on anyone that the rapid development and initial distribution of the COVID-19 vaccinations were a signature accomplishment of President Trump's administration. DeSantis himself was an early booster of the vaccines, even arranging an on-air inoculation of a World War II veteran on the air on FOX News. This, however, was before Trump's conduct from January 6 forward was aired in all its graphic detail.

While Trump in many opinion polls among Republican voters remains a favorite for the 2024 presidential nomination, that is not expected to hold--which opens the door for DeSantis. But, of course, there's absolutely no connection between DeSantis' ambition and this latest effort to justify his change of position on COVID vaccines.

This is most reminiscent of DeSantis' election police force that found about 20 convicted felons who voted anyway. Of course, DeSantis forgot to let us in on the fact that election officials told these people they were eligible to vote. Anyone know how many of these "fraudulent" voters were convicted of this horrible crime? Zero. Nada.

But that's not what's most important to DeSantis; he made a spectacle of arresting these people, the result is that eligible voters shied away from voting this past November, and may decide it's not worth the aggravation of voting in the future. Which, of course, suits DeSantis and his minions just fine. Suppress the vote of the opposition; feed the masses with conspiracy theories based on the most gossamer of information that can easily be spun to his advantage. Keep them angry and ignorant; that's the plan.

Something else DeSantis told the Supreme Court: "The Biden Administration and pharmaceutical corporations continue to push widespread distribution of (COVID) vaccines on the public, including children as young as 6 months old, through relentless propaganda while ignoring real-life adverse events."

The circle is now complete. Those expecting a fair and impartial grand jury probe are only fooling themselves. This is an inquiry with the results already known.

The purpose of this grand jury investigation is to gather evidence to support DeSantis' view that the Biden Administration and the pharmaceutical companies conspired to convince the public that vaccines were safe and necessary to help defeat a raging COVID pandemic.

His supporters stand ready, willing and able to buy it. Conspiracy theories are the right wing's stock in trade. The rest see through this his latest charade.

MITCH MCCONNELL IS LOOKING FOR A FEW QUALITY SENATE CANDIDATES

Senate Minority Leader Mitch McConnell has placed the blame for the Republican Party's less than stellar showing in the November midterm elections squarely on Donald Trump, saying that because of him, the party had "candidate quality" issues that cost Republicans the United States Senate. McConnell vowed the party would do a better job recruiting quality candidates for the senate in 2024.

Specifically, McConnell points to Kari Lake in Arizona and Herschel Walker in Georgia as the type of candidates who were not of sufficient quality. What he really means is that they, and a few others, were an embarrassment to party leaders, even those who have their own history of saying and doing embarrassing things.

Trump, of course, denies McConnell's charge and blames McConnell for his poor efforts in generating funds and support for several of Trump's handpicked candidates.

It's interesting—actually, funny--to see party leaders who pride themselves on personal accountability do everything they can to avoid taking ownership of their own contributions to their party's losses. They are far more interested in finger-pointing than standing up and saying "we screwed up because so many of our candidates couldn't pass the giggle test. We need candidates who can put together coherent sentences and actually demonstrate that they understand the issues." Getting an honest appraisal is daunting; at least McConnell is showing some effort toward this end. Whether he stays the course on this, of course, remains to be seen. He is known for flip-flopping on Trump depending on which way the wind is blowing at the time.

The first thing that must be realized in solving any problem is to admit there is one. No one in the Republican Party was vocal enough—or honest enough—to admit early on that candidate selection was a serious problem. Too many thought that the Republican brand and Democrat-bashing were enough. Wrong. Now, with the election cycle over, comes the classic blame game. The party leadership's message: blame anybody but me.

How exactly will McConnell find better candidates than those offered by Trump? McConnell will soon be 81. He is entering the age of dotage, and certainly needs help in his efforts to find top-quality candidates for the high office of United States senator.

So, let me offer some advice as he begins his search.

First, Mitch, ditch the election liars and election deniers. Those who still believe Trump won the election and that it was stolen from him are becoming fewer and fewer. Of course, there will always be a number of folks who deny reality, keep their heads in the sand, and believe Trump is the vicar of all that is truth. That number, however, will never elect a president and will have a harder and harder time electing a senator as more and more of Trump's collisions with the law come to focus.

By the time the 2024 campaign season rolls around, Trump's prospects might lean more to the jail house than the White House, so you would be wise, Mitch, to steer clear of this impending disaster.

Second, ditch the conspiracy theorists and uncertified crazies. Remember Rep. Marjorie Taylor Greene's accusation that Jewish space lasers were trying to shoot down Santa at the North Pole? You might be able to carry a congressional district with a weirdo like her, but a senate seat? I don't think so. How about the 2016 Pizzagate nonsense, highlighted when a 28-year-old man was arrested for walking into a Washington, D.C., pizza joint with an assault rifle, saying he wanted to investigate claims that the restaurant was running a pedophile ring from its basement with the help of Bill and Hillary Clinton? Mitch, your party doesn't need this to win elections.

As you search for quality candidates, go with the party's usual talking points: limited government, less taxes, personal responsibility, Mitch. People lap up that stuff, so long as they don't match those words with actions. I suggest actually making sure the party's deeds match those words.

Limited government doesn't mean cracking down on academic freedom or suppressing education curriculum; that's the kind of heavy-handed government Republicans are supposed to oppose.

Less taxes means just that; for everyone, not just the rich. If tax cuts are to be permanent, make them permanent for everyone. Just make sure there's enough revenue flowing into the treasury to pay for programs that benefit the majority of Americans, instead of the wealthy few.

I don't have to say any more about personal responsibility. Stop the blame game. Get to work doing the people's business; goodness knows we have enough problems to deal with without engaging in culture wars and woke attacks. Remember, Mitch, the opposite of woke is ignorance.

And cut the socialism stuff, Mitch. We've had socialist-type programs since the 1930s. This attack against the Democrats didn't help in this year's election, and you have some in your party who continue to support Russia's dictator Vladimir Putin, who remains the poster boy for socialism and communism.

Third, vet candidates much more carefully. You've got a Rep.-elect, George Santos, who seemingly has a way of appearing well qualified and experienced—but if it's all a lie, that doesn't help the recruiting process. Santos said he will have a complete explanation next week. He most likely needs time to try to make lemonade out of lemons. If his story—or resume—doesn't hold up, let your buddy Kevin McCarthy know Santos will be an albatross around the party's neck, and it may be advisable to secure his resignation before he has any further chances of making things up. We know incessant lying can be dangerous;

even leading to violence. You remember January 6, don't you Mitch?

Fourth, consider which current senators are quality officials who can serve as models for your selection process. How about Josh Hawley of Missouri? He was the one who pumped his fists in support of the January 6 insurrectionists, only to be seen a short time later running for his life from the same mob he supported. Probably not a good choice here.

What about Ted Cruz? Didn't he flee to Cancun when the weather turned bad in Texas last year? This certainly doesn't show good judgment. He's certainly well-educated, but we all know that there's a difference between being well-educated and actually learning important lessons. Teachers can teach; whether a student learns is a completely different matter. Seems there's a lot of that in your party, Mitch.

There's a governor in Florida who has impeccable education credentials, but apparently hasn't learned much about how our democracy flourishes and survives. Restricting liberty and calling it freedom might work, but only for a while. Remember, you can fool all of the people some of the time, and some of the people all the time, but you can't fool all of the people all of the time. Take note, Mitch. Sooner or later, people do wake up; they do see the forest through the trees.

Mitch, your search recalls that of Diogenes, the Greek philosopher in search for an honest man. You may have great difficulty in your search; in fact, it may prove impossible, but at least you're prepared to reject the lunacy and nonsense that has gripped your party for several years now.

You are prepared, right? And others will follow your lead here, right?

"NOT GUILTY BY REASON OF INSANITY."

"I've done nothing wrong."

Donald Trump repeated this line over and over again as he railed against the House Select January 6 Committee's final report referring four criminal charges to the Department of Justice and taking Trump over the coals for his many transgressions.

To the charge of inciting an insurrection by firing up a mob to attack the capital in order to prevent the certification of the election results: "I've done nothing wrong."

To the charge that he sat watching the insurrection on television for hours before telling his rioters to go home, they're patriots and he loves them: "I've done nothing wrong."

To the charge that he would see that a letter is sent to state officials falsely saying the Justice Department believed state legislatures had sufficient justification to select new electors: "I've done nothing wrong."

To the charge that Trump conspired with others to submit slates of fake electors to Congress and the National Archives: "I've done nothing wrong."

To the charge of intimidating state officials to "find" sufficient votes to elect him at all costs: "I've done nothing wrong."

And to the charge of taking classified government records from the White House and strewing them around his Mar-a-Lago estate, once again we heard his pitiful refrain: "I've done nothing wrong."

Of course, Trump will never utter the words "I've done nothing wrong" under oath in a court of law.

And that really doesn't matter.

Those who observed Trump's actions on January 6; witnessed the mass of evidence and testimony from Republicans during the televised committee hearings; read at least part of the massive report by that committee damning him conduct; heard his feckless defense to stealing government records (he can declassify just by thinking about it), believe that it's insane for him to claim he did nothing wrong.

And that's precisely the point! This is exactly what he wants the American public to believe.

We should have seen this was coming. After all, Trump always fancied himself as a stable genius; smarter than all of his military and civilian advisors; smarter than all his cabinet officers—heck, he'll tell anyone the smartest man in the world! Just ask him. And he's already proclaimed himself the greatest president in American history! No one asked him that. Nevertheless, he's a true legend in his own mind.

Only he would be smart enough, clever enough and shrewd enough to come up with such a great plan.

This is his Plan A if he is criminally charged.

By repeating over and over again ad infinitum ad nauseam that he "did nothing wrong" in the face of overwhelming evidence to the contrary, Trump's lawyers will plead their client not guilty by reason of insanity!

There is an analogy applicable here. FOX News mouthpiece Tucker Carlson successfully defended a defamation action against him when a judge appointed by Trump concluded that "any reasonable viewer" doesn't actually believe what Carlson is saying to be true. It is therefore unreasonable to take what Tucker Carlson says as truth.

If one of Trump's favorite TV personalities can avoid legal accountability by saying no reasonable person can believe him, why can't Carlson's favorite president say that, by babbling incessantly that he did nothing wrong, he's insane?

Think about this. If a judge (perhaps even one appointed by Trump himself), accepts the defense that Trump's belief demonstrates he's out of touch with reality, Trump can be assigned to his estate where he can live his life in luxury and never be held criminally accountable for his actions. He'll get some form of counseling, but otherwise have a joyous ride into senility.

All because of a brilliantly concocted plan to simply say he did nothing wrong—again and again and again..... !

THIS IS NOT THE CHRISTMAS SPIRIT; THIS IS A CRUEL AND HEARTLESS ACT

Christmas is a time for reflection, hope, sharing, giving, love and goodwill toward all. But not everyone believes this. Busloads of migrants were dropped off outside of Vice President Kamala Harris' home in frigid weather. Some of the migrants were wearing only T-shirts to shelter them from the bitter cold.

We don't know who's responsible for this Christmas Eve act of heartlessness, but we do know that three Republican arch-conservative governors--Greg Abbott of Texas, Doug Ducey of Arizona and Ron DeSantis of Florida--have sent migrants to other states by bus and airplane.

Whatever one's view of our nation's immigration policies may be, there are those the words etched on the Statue of Liberty; the words that begin with "Give me your tired, your poor, your huddled masses yearning to breathe free." Words matter. Well, at least to most Americans.

Conservatives press their beliefs in family values. We hear repeatedly about the need to preserve traditional conservative values. George Bush spoke often about compassionate conservatism.

The questions thus arise: Is this act of shipping migrants to the cold clime on Christmas Eve without so much as some blankets to keep them warm an act of compassionate conservatism?

Is this what conservatives mean by traditional American values?

At a time when peace on earth and goodwill toward all is supposed to be the message, is this dropping off of migrants in frigid weather an example of what they mean by conservative values?

And what specific conservative value is demonstrated by this act?

To me, it looks like cruel, inhumane, callous, heartless treatment of the most vulnerable of people under the most vulnerable of circumstances.

At least the anonymous sender could have offered some hot tea or a few blankets.

Remember the three main characters in the Wizard of Oz? One searching for a brain, another a heart and the third courage? Well, someone who would act so cruelly has no heart, lacks courage and doesn't have much for a brain.

But at least this vile act gives pause when some folks pat themselves on the back over how compassionate and caring they say they are.

UNHINGED AND DERANGED. AND NOT WORTH THE EFFORT

This is one of several statements offered by Donald Trump as his Christmas cheer on his laughably euphemistic truth social:

"Merry Christmas to EVERYONE, including the Radical Left Marxists that are trying to destroy our Country, the Federal Bureau of Investigation that is illegally coercing & paying Social and LameStream Media to push for a mentally disabled Democrat over the Brilliant, Clairvoyant, and USA LOVING Donald J. Trump, and, of course, The Department of Injustice, which appointed a Special 'Prosecutor' who, together with his wife and family, HATES 'Trump' more than any other person on earth. LOVE TO ALL!"

This is not the language of a rational person. This is rage at our democratic institutions for daring to hold him accountable for his deviant behavior.

He is hoping that his dwindling number of rabid supporters will do what others did on January 6—take to the streets and attack our symbols of Democracy. Hundreds of those who did precisely that currently are spending this year's holidays—and many will spend future holidays—behind bars for foolishly believing Trump's lies and that he truly cares for them. They have learned the hard way what so many others knew before that fateful day—Trump cares only for himself. He uses people like pawns, existing only to serve his overinflated ego. Woe to those who disagree with him, as so many have learned to their great regret.

Regardless, he's now hoping enough people refuse to learn from history and will take up his cause and defend the indefensible. Like every other person accused of breaking the law, he'll be entitled to due process as guaranteed by the Constitution. He'll have the right to a trial by a jury of his peers. He'll have the right to be confronted by those witnesses who have relevant evidence against him, and have the right to cross examine all who testify against him. And he will be given every opportunity to state his position in the same manner as those who testify against him—under oath and before a court of law. He will also have the right against self-incrimination, which means he can choose to remain silent.

Trump really doesn't want anything to do with the criminal justice system. He's hoping to intimidate Department of Justice officials into not filing charges, either those stemming from January 6 and surrounding events as graphically set out in the House committee's devastating final report, or resulting from his theft of government records and his mishandling of them at his estate.

Prosecutors, however, are a tough lot, and they don't intimidate so easily. Just as the House committee wasn't intimidated by Trump's bluster, so neither will the Department of Justice prosecutors.

Failing of his own efforts at intimidation, Trump is hoping that his unveiled threat of violence by his blind loyalists will prevent public officials from doing their job as their oaths and the Constitution command. Again, these officials are not easily intimidated—as he will find out soon enough.

As for those who might do Trump's bidding and consider violent acts against those identified in his quoted rant, just recall what happened to those who chose violence on January 6. Those insurrectionists wallowing in jail learned a harsh lesson: Trump simply isn't worth the price they are paying for their actions. He really doesn't care about them.

Trump is psychologically and emotionally damaged goods. His support among elected officials is dropping, and those who would dare to consider a repeat of January 6 well know what the consequences would be.

He and he alone is responsible for his actions. His "I did nothing wrong" defense would be laughable were it not coming from a former president of the United States. His time to face the criminal justice system draws near.

HONORED CONSERVATIVES OR A ROGUES' GALLERY?

In 2016, then-presidential candidate Donald Trump said: "The mob takes the Fifth Amendment. If you're innocent, why are you taking the Fifth Amendment?"

A perfectly logical question. Why seek protection from self-incrimination if there is nothing to hide?

That question should be asked of Trump himself, who plead the Fifth often and has never testified to a single fact under oath.

Others in his circle have taken the Fifth rather than disclose information that might incriminate them. They include: Kash Patel, Eric Trump, John Eastman, Roger Stone, Alex Jones, Jeffrey Clark, Michael Flynn, Kelli Ward, Jenna Ellis, Kenneth Chesebro, Phil Waldron, Bianca Garcia, Julie Fancelli, and Charlie Kirk. As more transcripts of the House January 6 committee are publicized, there is no doubt other names will be added to this list.

Then there are those Trump loyalists who asked for preemptive pardons just in case they did something wrong: Mark Meadows, Rudy Giuliani, Andy Biggs, Mo Brooks, Matt Gaetz, Marjorie Taylor Greene, Louis Gohmert, Scott Perry and John Eastman. Five on this list are current members of Congress. This list as well may grow as more information is publicly disclosed.

Why ask for a pardon if they did nothing that might be criminal?

Then there are those four members of the House whose conduct revealed them to be ethically challenged, at best. They are Kevin McCarthy, Jim Jordan, Andy Biggs and Scott Perry. McCarthy is slated to become speaker of the House; Jordan is in line to become chairman of the House Judiciary Committee.

Recall that McCarthy and Jordan also refused to honor congressional subpoenas and have already said they will investigate everything Biden and others in his administration. They will not consider their own ethical behavior, or why they refused to honor subpoenas. As their leader said, why refuse if there is nothing to hide?

Republicans need to ask themselves if these men and women represent Republican conservatism of the highest order steeped in respect for the rule of law and Democratic institutions; or are they merely political hacks who are part of a Republican rogues' gallery. Democrats and many Republicans know the answer; they want to see if the blind loyalists are finally waking up.

IMMIGRATION: A PHILOSOPHICAL DIVIDE
WITH MIGRANTS AS PAWNS

Once again, the dispute over immigration has reared its ugly head. Republicans rail at Democrats for the humanitarian crisis at our nation's southern border. Democrats blast Republicans as cruel and heartless for sending busloads of migrants to the cold clime with only T-shirts protecting them from the bitter weather.

Each side is claiming the high ground as thousands are mere pawns in what is an ongoing ideological struggle.

The history of immigration is the history of America.

Whether driven by poverty or war, immigrants have always flocked to our shores seeking a better life. America was, for them, the land of opportunity. Whether those doors were always open, however, is another matter. The history of immigration has its highs as well as its lows.

We know there were times when immigrants were welcomed here. Those days seem to be in the past. To be sure, there are reasons supporting both sides in this debate. Uncontrolled migration has its consequences, but so does a "send them all back" policy; sending migrants back home will only result in further efforts by them to enter our country. Putting them in jail accomplishes their purpose of living in America.

As vital as this issue is to all concerned, as important as immigration has been to the growth and development of our nation, the question naturally arises: why can't our elected leaders come up with a sound plan that globally addresses immigration in all of its manifestations?

The differences between Republicans and Democrats over this issue, and why stalemate and inertia govern the day, are thrashed out in numerous articles and books. What is most interesting, however, are the areas of overlap between the two parties. Perhaps someday cooler heads will prevail and they will pass comprehensive immigration legislation.

Putting it in capsule form, however, is the overriding fact that Republicans see immigration as a critical threat to the country, believe restricting immigration makes America safer, and support using troops to stop migrants from crossing into the United States from the south. They further seek to end asylum as we know it, end Deferred Action for Childhood Arrivals (DACA), which grants a work permit and protection from deportation to children brought to America by undocumented parents, and restrict legal immigration.

Democrats, on the other hand, don't consider immigration a critical threat, seek to continue accepting asylum seekers, extend a path to citizenship for DACA recipients, and reform our legal immigration system.

What is certain is that our elected leaders can't continue to kick this can down the road. Sooner rather than later, there will be a time of reckoning.

REPUBLICAN PARTY LEADERS REMAIN SILENT IN THE FACE OF THIS LATEST EMBARRASSMENT

It shouldn't really come as a surprise that George Santos was elected to Congress by conning enough voters in his district with lies and deceit. The Republican Party, after all, has as its leader a former president who is a pathological liar and master con artist. Santos figures if it worked for Trump, why wouldn't it work for him?

And no one should be surprised at the silence of party leaders to this latest embarrassment, a sharp slap in the face to what was once a respectable political party.

These leaders are silent because if Santos is forced to resign, another election would have to be held in that district, and the voters there might not take too kindly to being fooled by another charlatan. To the House Republicans, their majority status is all that matters.

One columnist said Santos "will be a real test of today's Republican Party. Does honesty and integrity matter at all? Or is GOP leadership so power-hungry that it will allow a serial fabulist to remain in office despite deceiving the public – and the voters who elected him – about key aspects of his biography?"

The answer to this question should be obvious: in today's sad excuse for the Republican Party, power trumps (pun intended) honesty and integrity.

Is Santos remorseful for his con game? Hardly. To the lies about his academic and employment status, he said he was sorry for embellishing his resume, but shrugged it off by saying "We do stupid things in life." First, there was no embellishment here; what he said were flat-out lies. Second, this wasn't a stupid mistake; this was a planned effort to deceive voters over the several months of a political campaign.

Santos was similarly dismissive of reporting on his false claims of Jewish heritage. "I never claimed to be Jewish. I am Catholic. Because I learned my maternal family had a Jewish background, I said I was 'Jew-ish.'" There is nothing funny or cute about his cavalier response to having his hand caught in the cookie jar. This is a dark stain on the House of Representatives, and a slap in the face to the truth, which is in diminishing supply in today's Republican Party.

We learned from the master con artist who currently resides in Mar-a-Lago that once a person makes it a habit of lying, there is no turning back. The lie becomes the truth, and a pathological liar will use every psychological technique to gaslight the public, causing them to question their own reality.

This is how gaslighting works. History is clear that dictators and despots are masters of deceit. It was Hitler's minister

Joseph Goebbels who said a lie repeated often enough becomes the truth.

Too many in the Republican Party are taking Goebbels' teaching to heart.

Over the past six years, the dominant wing of the Republican Party has morphed into one taken over by pathological liars, conspiracy theorists, bigots, election deniers, ethically barren, and scofflaws who don't have the words honesty or integrity in their vocabularies. Now we can add another con artist to this growing rogues' gallery that is the party leadership.

Instead of remorse or shame, party leaders double down and accuse those who point out these failings of engaging in witch hunts, relying on "fake news," etc. We're all too familiar with their blame game. It's supposed to deflect, but as with any lie repeated too long, people grow tired and eventually get turned off to the nonsensical noise.

With the growing disenchantment and downright disgust of what the Republican Party has become, this can't happen soon enough.

No, Santos is correct in saying he's not a criminal—at least, not yet. An investigation into his finances, especially his taxes, may prove otherwise. Right now, he's just a serial liar. And Republican officials were aware of his multiple lies. This proves he'll be right at home in today's version of the Republican Party.

As if the party can't get any wackier, far right wingers Marjorie Taylor Greene and Lauren Boebert are at each other's throats, and Greene is on the outs with others on the far right for not being extreme enough over who will be House speaker.

And then there's their party leader, who shows how crazy crazy can be with his daily rants from Mar-a-Lago.

Are Republicans proud of their party?

Republican Party leaders can choose to meet these revelations of repeated lies with silence, but prosecutors are using a classic line that will be this guy's undoing: follow the money. Since Santos has lied about everything that qualifies a person to be elected to Congress, what are the sources of his income? And where did he get $700,000 to loan his campaign? And then there are those tax returns.

This is a black eye for a party that has lots of them. Republicans in Congress don't need another. Not that this one bothers them.

LET THEM HELP RE-ELECT JOE BIDEN

Today, after Donald Trump fought vigorously for several years to prevent the public from seeing his tax returns, those returns are now available for all to see. Predictably, his congressional lackeys vow revenge by promising to fight for the release of tax returns for Democrat Presidents

Carter, Clinton, Obama and Biden. Wait, every president since Richard Nixon disclosed their tax returns.

Trump was the only outlier. Until today. Others disclosed voluntarily; Trump resisted. No revenge factor here for party extremists.

As for revenge, Trump's loyalists will have to search for another source as tax returns are off the table.

Perhaps their revenge will be the launching of investigations into Biden and his son. Oh, wait. They've already promised to do that.

Maybe they'll issue a subpoena to President Biden himself. We know what will happen then...more years of litigation.

It would be well to remember that, just as is the case with the January 6 committee, a congressional committee can't bring criminal charges. Regardless of what crumbs the House finds, anything that smacks of criminal charges have to be turned over to the Department of Justice...which for the next two years at least falls under the Biden Administration.

And if things get really hairy, remember the president has one power that isn't subject to review by the courts. It's called the pardon power.

So, it would be wise for Messrs. Kevin McCarthy, Jim Jordan, and other wild-eyed House members bent on revenge to remember that the Democrats run the executive branch of government. And there isn't a thing they can do about it for at least until 2025.

The public awaits action on important issues affecting all Americans while all the Republican Party extremists promise is revenge politics.

The party's base will believe anything these rabid ranters say; the majority, however, know the game they're playing and see through their smoke and mirrors.

It would also be wise for them to remember what happened in 1994 when Newt Gingrich launched his attack on Bill Clinton. He and his newly elected right wing followers thought they hit pay dirt with the challenge to Clinton and extreme Contract for America. The extremist movement, however, proved too much for the voters and helped catapult Clinton to a second term.

So, let today's Republican Party leaders investigate to their heart's content. Let the public grow tired of their shenanigans. Let the public see how extreme the party has become. They won't learn the lessons history teaches; they believe they're smarter than everyone else.

As they did with Clinton, let them help re-elect Joe Biden.

BITS AND PIECES:

Biden's Legislative Record for Two Years is Better than Trump's for Four.

Trump loyalists believe their leader accomplished more as president than anyone. President Biden signed five major pieces of legislation into law in 2022: climate, health and tax laws; election laws to prevent a repeat of January 6; tough gun laws; laws to improve competition with China; and same-sex marriage law protection. In 2021, he signed the American Rescue Plan and Infrastructure and Jobs law, among others. That's seven major laws in two years.

Aside from the permanent tax cuts for the wealthy in 2017, what other major bills did Trump sign during his four years in office? Silence.

Voters Rejected Republican Party Extremism; Party Leaders Respond by Becoming More Extreme.

Let's see now. This past November, the national electorate generally said the Republican Party is a bit too extreme for their tastes. They sent many election deniers and Trump loyalists down to defeat. So, how does the Republican House leadership respond to these voters: by advocating for even more extremism.

The party is about to anoint such House flyweights as Jim Jordan and Marjorie Taylor Greene into leadership positions. There's even some chatter that Donald Trump is looking at Arizona election denier and Trump worshipper Kari Lake and Greene as a potential running mate.

2023 is already starting out on some crazy footing. And in the words of that great song by the Carpenters: they've only just begun.

Republicans Can't Choose a Speaker of the House, but They Can Embarrass Themselves.

The extreme wing of the Republican Party has put forth Rep. Byron Donalds of Florida for Speaker of the House as an alternative to Kevin McCarthy. Not to be outdone by the Democrats who've elected Rep. Hakeem Jeffries leader of the House Democratic Caucus, the nomination of Donalds by the most extreme members of the House Republican Party allows them to pat themselves and claim they judge not by the color of one's skin, but by the content of one's character. What would Martin Luther King, Jr., say about the Republican fiasco currently on display over the selection of a speaker?

Jeffries has served five terms in the House, including serving in leadership positions when the Democrats controlled the House. Donalds has served exactly one term in Congress. He has never served in a leadership position. In one of his first acts, he voted to object to the certification of electors from Arizona and Pennsylvania in the 2020 presidential election. Before election to Congress, Donalds served four years in the Florida House of Representatives during which he chaired the Insurance and Banking Subcommittee. With this skeletal background, the House extremists deem him qualified to be speaker and second in the line of succession to become President.

One other point. As a young man, Donalds was arrested for marijuana distribution; the charges were dropped as part of a pre-trial diversion program. In 2000, he pleaded guilty to a felony bribery charge as part of a scheme to defraud a bank, which was expunged after he entered the Florida House. Considering the election of George Santos who has a history of trouble with the truth, and the January 6 House committee report finding sufficient evidence for criminal charges to be brought against Donald Trump, and ethics issues against McCarthy and three other Republican House members, Donalds profile seems to fit right in.

It wasn't too long ago that we had a president with no government experience. We know how that worked out. Yet, for these few off-the-wall House members, one term on the back bench is ample qualifications to lead the United States House of Representatives and be second in line to the presidency.

There should be uniform sense of embarrassment over how these adults are behaving before a national audience. Sadly, only the members of one political party (and a few of the other who must remain silent lest they anger the shrill voices) are. I've seen high school and college governments function with more professionalism than what are witnessing from the House Republicans.

For Republicans, Immigration "Reform" is all About a Wall.

The other day, I saw a Facebook post that I found both sobering and sad. The subject was the upcoming holidays, and that people of varying faiths who will be visiting their places of worship in celebration and remembrance. The message was for those attending to be alert and use caution. The message is certainly a sobering one, considering the frequency of attacks on people who are considered "different" from the attackers.

But what saddened me is the number of posts that said if only Donald Trump had been allowed to finish his wall at the nation's southern border, none of these problems would exist. That's the key: in their mindset, it's these illegal aliens who are causing all these problems.

Sadly, this is categorically untrue. The nation's national security apparatus has made it abundantly clear that the most serious threat to our national security is right wing domestic violence: the kind we saw marching in Charlottesville, Va.; attack our nation's Capital on January 6; threaten the lives of the Speaker of the House, the former Vice President, Michigan's governor and others who dare challenge them; and those who utter baseless claims about Blacks, Jewish people, the gay community, and just about anyone else who's different.

We need more better angels to come forth and deal with fact, not opinion based on fear.

Tragedy on the Football Field.

Fans who tuned in to watch the recent Bills-Bengals football game witnessed a horrific incident instead. After what appeared to be a routine tackle, Bills safety Damar Hamlin got up, and then collapsed. The looks on the faces of the players, coaches and fans made clear the seriousness of the situation. Hamlin, 24, went into cardiac arrest. After the medics restored his heartbeat on the field, he was taken to a nearby hospital where he remains in critical condition.

This brought to mind a tragedy that occurred in the NFL more than 50 years ago. During a game against the Chicago Bears at Tiger Stadium on October 24, 1971, Detroit Lions wide receiver Chuck Hughes was heading back to his team's huddle after a play when he collapsed, clutching his chest. He was taken off the field in an ambulance and rushed to a nearby hospital where he was pronounced dead. Following his death, it was discovered that Hughes had a family history of heart problems and that one of his arteries was 75% clogged. Hughes is the only NFL player to die during a football game.

In hockey, the only NHL player to die during a game was Bill Masterson. It happened in 1968 when Minnesota North Stars' Masterson, 29, collided with two players and fell to the ice in such a way that his head took the full force of the fall. This was before helmets were required. Each year, the NHL gives out the Bill Masterson Award "to the player who best exemplifies the qualities of perseverance, sportsmanship, and dedication to hockey."

The only major league baseball player to die during a game was Cleveland Indians' Ray Chapman, who was hit in the head by a pitch in 1920, well before batting helmets were required. He was 29.

There is no record of any NBA players dying during a game.

HOUSE REPUBLICANS ARE IN SEARCH OF A SPEAKER WHILE DONORS ARE CONCERNED WITH THE PARTY LOOKING "STUPID."

Republicans are hearing from party donors and constituents that the party "looks stupid" in selecting a speaker. Seems party leaders should have been concerned about looking stupid for the last few years. If I wanted to see a circus, I'd go to a real one, instead of watching these clowns embarrass themselves.

I think things were better in the old days, and I hope it's not an age thing with me. I don't recall much discussion about policies lately; it seems the House Republicans are more bent on investigations than in actually governing. I haven't heard any sensible legislative proposals that benefit most Americans, and I haven't heard how they plan to get legislation passed through the Senate and signed by Biden. They can pass stuff out of the House until hell freezes over, but unless they have a plan that involves the Senate and Biden, they have accomplished nothing.

McCarthy, should he become speaker, has promised accountability, but for whom? Certainly not for Trump and his band of lemmings. He means accountability for all thing Biden. And if they can drag Fauci, the January 6 committee members, and Biden's cabinet into the fray, all the better for them, so they believe. I can't bring myself to refer to this group as the GOP. The Republican Party today isn't grand and isn't old; it's a captive of extremists that lacks courage, and don't show much brains or heart, either.

SOME THOUGHTS ON FACT VS. BELIEF

The other day at my senior men's club meeting, the subject of religion came up. I was asked whether I attended services during the holidays; I said I didn't and that I'm not a fan of organized religion.

When asked why, I related my experiences where, so long as my wife and I gave what was considered our "fair share," we were welcomed with open arms. But as soon as other financial obligations necessitated reducing our "fair share," we were treated like outcasts. It seems that money is too important a function of organized religion.

My second reason stems from the prayer given each week seeking forgiveness for the previous week's transgressions. Following services, we're convinced that we've been forgiven, only to return the following week to repeat the same prayer seeking forgiveness for that week's transgressions. I thought what a wonderful way it is to be forgiven for whatever machinations committed between each service. This just struck me as such a convenient way to brush off transgressions; too convenient for my fact-driven background.

I don't think I should have to pay to sit in a building with others and seek forgiveness. If I do something wrong, I think it's perfectly fine to ask for forgiveness at that point. Along this line, it shouldn't be necessary to ask for forgiveness in the first place. Just follow the Golden Rule and do unto others as they would do unto you. Sounds reasonable to me.

I think much of one's view of religion is based on background. Religion is belief-based. My professional education, training and experience—briefly in journalism and extensively in law—are fact-based. You can argue facts; lawyers do this in court every day. So much of the legal profession is based on the ability to marshal facts into a persuasive argument which, when applied to the law, leads to a favorable conclusion.

Religion, however, is largely dependent on belief; belief in scripture; text, dogma, religious history, etc. Because belief is so personal, it's not wise to argue belief.

There is no question of the power of religion. My wife and I have been most fortunate to having visited the Vatican, Westminster Abbey, Notre Dame in Paris and Montreal, the Blue Mosque and Hagia Sophia in Istanbul, Church of the Savior on Spilled Blood in St. Petersburg, Russia; and others. We've seen the ruins of the ancient Temples of Zeus, Poseidon, Isis, etc. Some of the most spectacular buildings in the world are erected and dedicated to religion.

French Sociologist Emile Durkheim identified three major functions of religion: "Religion unites people, promoting social cohesion; it encourages people to obey cultural norms, promoting conformity; it gives meaning and purpose to life." Some, however, believe that Karl Marx was correct when he said religion is the opium of the masses, designed more for control than to educate and give meaning and purpose to life. This is a debate as old as religion itself and will persist as long as there is civilization. For me, religion is, as Durkheim notes, whatever people find in the teachings that give peace, comfort, and solace to the followers.

Problems arise, however, when followers of one religion believe their religion is superior to all others, and seek to impose their beliefs on others.

A further problem is when religious leaders are discovered to be less than what they appear to be, more out to make millions off their true believers than to adhere to Durkheim's view.

I recall a book written more than 40 years ago entitled "Give Me That Prime-Time Religion" by Jerry Sholes. It told the story of Oral Roberts, a nationally famous evangelist-faith healer, who claimed to have based his ministry on providing spiritual succor to thousands of needy, hopeful individuals who turned to him for healing and religious leadership; yet actually functioned to enrich him and to build large-scale monuments to his ego. Their faith in him allowed Roberts to build a personal empire of astonishing wealth and influence.

I also recall Jimmy Swaggart, a prominent televangelist several years ago, who vigorously preached against sin, only to be outed when caught with a prostitute. After being caught, he appeared on his TV show bawling his eyes out screaming "I have sinned." It was a bravado performance.

More recently, other televangelists have been caught up in one scandal or another, including Jim Bakker, Franklin Graham, Pat Robertson and Joel Osteen.

There is no doubt these men, as well as many others, are outstanding speakers who have the ability to connect with their followers. They are motivators; they are persuaders. But they have accumulated extreme wealth that, to many, can be unsettling or disturbing. After all, Jesus Christ had neither material wealth nor a great cathedral from which to preach. Religion must never become "do as I say, not as I do."

As we were discussing these matters, another thought came to mind—an explanation why Donald Trump's lawyers lost so badly in court following the 2020 election. His lawyers rushed into court with plenty of beliefs, but no facts. Even those election deniers from this past November went into court armed with beliefs, but no facts. That's why they lost.

In a court of law, beliefs will not carry the day. Courts apply facts to law. Our entire judicial system is predicated on this single reality. Facts must be observable; they can't be based on surmise or conjecture. Lawyers may well argue over the significance of a fact, and how that fact might apply to the law. Ultimately, however, the court will make findings of fact that control the case, and apply those facts to the law. This encapsulates how our judicial system functions.

Beliefs are subjective; facts are objective. This is a quantum difference. We can agree on fact; I doubt we will never have uniform agreement on belief.

In our daily lives, there is room for belief and fact. One doesn't replace the other. So much of the tension between the two involves knowing when to rely on one as opposed to the other.

The consequences of supplanting fact with belief should be obvious: one stark consequence will be the destruction of our judicial system.

NEW YEAR'S RESOLUTONS AND BUCKET LISTS

The other day, I mentioned in a Facebook post that I don't make New Year's resolutions; never have and never will.

Today, a couple of friends asked what my resolutions are, and what items I have on my bucket list.

It seems that most people make New Year's resolutions, and have this list of things they want to do before they meet their Maker.

Because it seems expected for folks to make resolutions, I did a bit of research and found the most common resolutions in order of importance are: exercise more, lose weight, get organized, learn a new skill or hobby, live life to the fullest (whatever that means), save more money and spend less money, quit smoking or drinking, spend more time with family and friends, travel more, and read more.

Over the past several days, I noticed lots of people signing up at my gym. Health-related issues are the most prominent New Year's resolutions. Getting in better shape, eating better and dieting are certainly noble things to strive for. But if past years is any indication, those signing up will attend a few sessions and then pay their monthly dues for non-attendance. Health clubs make lots of money off people who pay dues but never show up.

In fact, the annual rite of resolutions-making is an exercise in futility. Recent studies show 43% of all people expect to fail before February, and almost one out of four quit within the first week of setting their New Year's resolutions. Most people quit before the end of January, and only 9% see their resolutions through successfully. The statistics break down as follows:

- 9% successfully keep their New Year's resolutions.
- 23% of people quit by the end of the first week, 64% after the first month and 81% before the end of the second year.
- Most people quit on the second Friday of the month, according to Strava, a Running and Cycling tracking app. They named this day "Quitters Day".
- 43% of people expect to give up on their goals by February, which explains the relatively high quitting rate in January.

Given this high rate of failure, the question naturally arises: Why do New Year's resolutions fail? They fail primarily due to timing. Most people are not ready to commit to their resolutions and give up because they either lose motivation, have not prioritized their goals, or swap their resolutions for newer, more relevant and readily achievable personal goals.

- 35% of people attribute losing motivation as the top reason for giving up, followed by being too busy (19%) and changing their goals and priorities (18%).
- The main reason why people fail is the timing of New Year's resolutions. While people want to achieve change, they have yet to be ready to commit fully.
- Successful individuals reported more stimulus control and willpower. Social support and interpersonal strategies became important after the first six months of pursuing the goal.
- Successful individuals are likely to experience 14 slip-ups during a two-year interval, indicating that

resilience or the ability to bounce back from setbacks is essential for goal success.

The problem with New Year's resolutions is that this end-of-year ritual becomes nothing more than a convenient excuse for what should be, for the most part, lifestyle choices made at any time the need arises. The point here is that this ritual becomes a crutch—and a very weak one at that--for decisions that should much more realistically be made during the ordinary course of one's life.

If someone is out of shape, overweight, etc., the time to do something about it is now, not at the end of the year. The same can be said for vowing to get one's finances in order, quit smoking or drinking, develop a new skill or hobby, or anything else a person might want to add to a list for an upcoming year. Chances are if a person sees a need, but decides to wait until the time is ripe to make a New Year's resolution, the result will be failure, as the above statistics graphically point out.

The statistics are most illustrative that making New Year's resolutions is a prescription for failure.

Then there's the bucket list, a list of the things that a person would like to do or achieve before they die. Research shows there are several types of bucket lists: marriage and family, personal development, career, travel, bucket lists for couples, etc. Just about anything in life can be added to one's bucket list.

I have a strong aversion to the phrase "bucket list." I prefer to think in terms of experiences or achievements that I hope to have or accomplish. It goes without saying that these must be reached while I'm alive; there isn't a person alive who can accomplish anything after they're gone. A bucket list might be an interesting subject for discussion, but I can do without it.

I think those who have a bucket list are too focused on checking off an item rather than actually enjoying the experience itself by living in that moment. Put another way, too much importance is placed on accomplishing what's on the list rather than enjoying the experiences themselves. Recently, we spent two weeks in Greece and a few days in Istanbul. I thoroughly enjoyed the sights, sounds, food, etc., and never once thought how great it will be to rush home and cross off these countries from my list---because I don't have a list that requires items to be crossed off!!

I am blessed with a wonderful wife, two wonderful daughters who have wonderful husbands, and four wonderful grandchildren. Nothing makes me happier than to be with my family.

I have many friends, reasonably good health, activities that keep me engaged, and the good fortune to enjoy my retirement years after a rewarding career in two professions. This year, I will reach a milestone decade that allows me to reflect on a life well-lived while looking forward to more exciting and rewarding experiences. I couldn't ask for more.

I have visited over 30 countries and plan to visit several more this year. I've written eight books and am working on a ninth, and perhaps more. I am engaged in academic and travel activities with my senior group. I certainly have plans for the future, but I'm not going to rush to accomplish them solely to cross off lines on a list.

With each new country visited, I plan to enjoy the people, culture, food, sites, etc., as I have in my previous journeys. With each section of my next book, I plan to enjoy the experience of writing for its own sake, as I have in writing the other eight. But I won't get caught up losing sight of the rich value of these experiences just to check off another notation on a list.

I plan to live in the moment, do what needs to be done when it needs to be done, and reflect later on what I've accomplished. I don't need a resolution or list to accomplish that. And I don't think anyone really needs them either.

HOW IMPORTANT IS ONE'S REPUTATION?

American business magnate, investor and philanthropist Warren Buffett says a person can spend 20 years building a sterling reputation, only to ruin it in five minutes.

Buffett says: "We look for three things when we hire people. We look for intelligence, we look for initiative or energy, and we look for integrity. And if they don't have the latter, the first two will kill you, because if you're going to get someone without integrity, you want them lazy and dumb."

I would add that without integrity, intelligence and initiative will be wasted on destructive behavior.

As we begin a new year, it's worthwhile to reflect on life choices and whether one's reputation built over the years is a source of pride or regret.

An online search reveals the names of numerous rich and famous people who spent years building a sterling reputation, only to destroy it in a matter of moments.

In sports, there are no bigger names that Pete Rose, Barry Bonds and Roger Clemens. Their baseball statistics are certainly worthy of the Hall of Fame. Yet, each will most likely never be selected—at least during their lifetimes—for transgressions each committed off the field.

For Rose, he committed baseball's cardinal sin of betting on games. It is of no importance that he bet on his team to win; betting on baseball goes to the heart of the game's faithfulness to fair competition. Betting influences decision-making by questioning whether decisions are directed toward game strategy or making money by winning a bet.

For Bonds and Clemens, they are poster boys for the steroid era, when certain drugs were considered performance-enhancing by speeding recovery, adding strength, and generally giving a player an unfair edge.

When asked about these men, do you remember their on-field exploits, or their cheating ways? How important is their reputation to them and, more important, their families?

Bill Cosby was considered America's dad. His stage and TV career were exemplary. He was loved, admired and adored....until his proclivities caught up with him. He's now in his 80s, his reputation shattered. Do you remember his time as America's dad, or do you remember what he did that resulted in his downfall? How important is the Cosby name to him and his family?

Rudy Giuliani was America's mayor. As mayor of New York on 9/11, he rallied his citizens and spoke for the nation as we battled back from that heinous attack. Giuliani stood out as a true leader....until he got caught up in everything Trump. Now, he's become a laughingstock, facing many legal issues as he nears his eighth decade. How much of a solid reputation does the Giuliani name have now? Is he proud of his name, and is his family proud of the sullied reputation Giuliani will leave behind?

Donald Trump could have been content with being a reality TV star and the public's perception of him as a consummate businessman worth billions. Instead, ego and greed got the best of him. He wanted to be president in the worst way—and in that he wildly succeeded.

With his tax, business and financial records now exposed, his business acumen has taken a permanent hit. As president, his incessant lies, incitement of a riot, and theft of government records will cause him to be ranked by experienced and respected historians as the worst president in our nation's history. We don't know what the future holds for him, but with the several investigations already under way, and perhaps more to follow from his tax and financial records, the outlook is dim.

With his notoriety, some wealthy and dwindling base of supporters, he may be able to withstand the loss of reputation, but what about his son Barron? Note that his daughter Ivanka and her husband Jared have already distanced themselves from him. Not a happy family situation.

The list of athletes, entertainers and political figures who've destroyed their reputations is a lengthy one. Wesley Snipes, Lindsey Lohan, Chris Brown, Amber Heard, Mel Gibson, Kanye West (Ye), O. J. Simpson, Roseanne Barr, the list goes on and on. Perhaps they thought they could succeed where others failed. There is a tendency for people like this to believe they are smarter than their predecessors who committed various sins. They were proven wrong.

Whether it be through drugs, violence, bigotry, theft, whatever may be the vice, these and so many others tossed their reputations in the trash can. Some may have enough financially to get by; others not so fortunate must pay the price of a lifetime of hardship and struggles.

To be sure, some have tried to rehabilitate their sullied reputations. Bill Clinton certainly comes to mind. Whether he, or anyone else who pursues rehabilitation of one's reputation, is ultimately successful is in the eye of the beholder.

The key word is as Buffet notes: integrity.

I recall a story I was told many years ago. I don't know whether it's true, but it makes the point. The story is that an elderly man, on his deathbed, calls over to his grandson and says: "My dear grandson, I am at the end of my life. I have neither wealth nor fame; all I can give you is my good name. I gave it to your father and I am now giving it to you. I worked hard to make sure the family name was respected. Your father carries forth the family name with honor and admiration. I ask only one thing of you: carry forth the good family name. Make sure it remains respected and admired. Do nothing to sully or stain it. If you make sure the name continues to be admired and respected, you will have a good life, as will your children and grandchildren when you make the same request of them."

A message worth pondering as we start a new year.

WHAT DOES THE SCORE OF HOUSE REPUBLICANS REALLY WANT?

As the circus that is the selection of the next House speaker continues, the question devolves around what 20 of the most extreme right wing legislators really want. They've given Rep. Kevin McCarthy a list of "reforms" that he has, for the most part, agreed to; however, there are other things in the mix, including personality. Some just don't like McCarthy, and that won't change.

At its essence, these 20 who are so extreme as to be aptly described as to the right of Attila the Hun, want two things: influence and power. They want a seat at the decision-making table and they want not only to be heard, but to be obeyed. They want power to initiate and power to veto. They are chaos-driven, love conservative media publicity, and generally have a view of themselves as greater than their sheer numbers. They want the House Republican majority to kowtow to their demands and cater to their wishes.

In short, they want the House to function far differently than it has in the recent past, and they don't care if they have to shut down the government to accomplish their goals.

They aren't so much interested in policy as they are in blowing up political—and constitutional—norms, believing the end justifies the means.

If McCarthy eventually becomes speaker, he will be weaker than any of his predecessors going back to the early 20th century; he will be subject to a single member effectively asking for a vote of no-confidence. And that's just for starters.

If there is agreement on a consensus speaker, whoever that person is will face the wrath of the 20 upon any deviation from their demands—and the wrath of many others if he or she gives in to their demands. Seeking unity from 222 House members will be a daunting, perhaps impossible, task for the speaker.

The Democrats, on the other hand, are completely unified behind their leadership team, and are gleefully watching their Republican counterparts self-destruct, arguing that if they can't even select a speaker without rancor and disharmony, how are they going to govern when the House debates the real issues affecting all Americans?

The House Republicans have already made clear that investigations of all things Biden will be the main focus once they get their leadership act together. Hunter Biden has been investigated for tax and foreign lobbying by a Republican-appointed prosecutor for four years now; so far, nothing. Joe Biden has been in public office for 46 consecutive years and counting, without a sniff of scandal, yet these Republicans will look into the Afghanistan withdrawal, COVID response, and the southern border— implicating one cabinet officer. Then there's the FBI for daring to remove stolen government records from Mar-a-Lago, and the House January 6 committee for daring to investigate Donald Trump for his inciting an insurrection, among other things.

For the Republicans, revenge politics trumps addressing the people's needs. What they won't investigate, of course, is any misconduct by a Republican. That includes Trump for criminal acts, as well as McCarthy and Jim Jordan for ethical failings.

We are where we are because far right legislators over the past 25 or so years, convinced enough people to demonize the party that took us out of the Great Depression with an unprecedented infusion of social service legislation, and won World War II by ending conservative isolationists' neutrality through mobilization of industry toward the war effort.

The shift to the right started with Ronald Reagan, moved further to the right under Newt Gingrich, and became the calling card of Trump and Trumpism. It has reached the point where McCarthy, Jim Jordan, Margorie Taylor Greene, etc., are considered more moderate that Matt Gaetz, Lauren Boebert, etc. It's as if to be a real Republican these days, one has to out-crazy others, moving the party further and further to the right.

Is there an end game here? What will our government—and nation—look like in 10 or 20 years?

Martin Luther King, Jr., reminded us that "the arc of the moral universe is long, but it bends toward justice." How will justice be defined? And who will define it?

TWO YEARS AGO: THERE IS STILL DARKNESS

Today marks the second anniversary of one of the darkest days in our nation's history. Since that attack on the capital, there has been a superabundance of discussion and debate over the whys and wherefores of an insurrection born of a lie the sole purpose of which was to keep in power the loser of a presidential election.

Today, the Tallahassee Democrat published an article entitled "2 years after Jan. 6 riot, country remains divided. Panel reveals motives, but many don't believe it." The last five words lie at the heart of this political and philosophical divide.

For far too many, belief is fact. If they believe no crimes were committed on January 6 in Washington, a stack of facts piled to the top of the capital won't persuade them otherwise. This is not only sad, but dangerous; how do you engage in meaningful dialog with those who refuse to accept facts that conflict with their beliefs?

The danger of supplanting fact with belief is no more graphically–and tragically–demonstrated than in the Big Lie itself. The committee report is unalterably clear that Donald Trump was told repeatedly by his campaign staff, his Justice Department and his White House staff that there was no evidence of election fraud sufficient to change the outcome. Every court told him there was no such evidence. Yet he continued to fan the flames of violence with his persistent lies because he couldn't admit to himself that he lost the election. He was all about winning; to admit losing would ruin his legacy, so he told his advisors.

Had he told the truth, lives would have been saved, property would have been protected, and the orderly process of America's historic peaceful transfer of power would have been maintained. Trump showed what one person's deceit can do to the country. The danger of belief trumping fact could not be more profound.

I have a copy of the January 6 committee report; I'm about half-way through it. It is a damning document, replete with fact upon fact supporting every finding and conclusion. It is a detailed, carefully written history of what led up to the attack, what took place on that horrible day, and what occurred in the immediate aftermath. It was written for those who value our Democracy and want to preserve it, and to provide a blueprint of what must be done to avoid a repeat. It was written with an eye to history.

It was not written to change the minds of those who continue to believe that Donald Trump was the victim of a rigged election; that the people at the capital two years ago were just some overeager supporters engaging in legitimate political discourse; or that the committee report is nothing more than a litany of conspiracy theories, as Trump loyalist Roger Stone noted.

That committee report also notes something else; a dark and ominous stain on Florida–Florida leads the nation in the number of arrests arising out of that insurrection.

As the news article notes, and the report makes clear, Florida-based militant and far-right groups played a significant role in the rebellion.

The report cites the guilty verdict against Kelly Meggs, the leader of the Florida Oath Keepers chapter, for seditious conspiracy. During one of its televised committee hearings last year, the committee noted that Meggs "celebrated" Trump's call for a massive protest and rifled off "an encrypted Signal message to Florida Oath Keepers that President Trump 'wants us to make it WILD … He called us all to the Capitol and wants us to make it wild!!! … Gentlemen we are heading to DC pack your s***!!'"

The report also said Meggs' organization, as well as other extremist groups like Florida Guardians of Freedom, "were not operating in silos" and spoke of an "alliance" between the Oath Keepers, the Florida Three Percenters, and Florida Proud Boys leader Enrique Tarrio, who has been charged with seditious conspiracy.

Two other Florida notables mentioned in the committee report are Roger Stone and Michael Flynn, who were among the "more than 30 witnesses" that "exercised their Fifth Amendment privilege against self-incrimination and refused on that basis to provide testimony."

As the report makes clear, many of those arrested on and after January 6 now recognize that what they did was stupid and dangerous. They are remorseful and realize they were played by a master con artist and his mentally challenged acolytes. They believed, and they feel betrayed. Too bad they didn't realize what so many knew years before this tragic event.

As they sit in their jail cells, they have reached their moment of truth; it can only be hoped that others will, too, as the arc of accountability and justice bends toward them.

Instead of Florida's leaders recognizing the state's role as embarrassing and hurtful to Florida's reputation, far right elements are actually doubling down and imposing more restrictive measures—all in the name of freedom, of course.

Laws limiting academic freedom, sanitizing history to avoid teachings that affect personal comfort, and the latest--to eliminate diversity training--are all designed to tamp down on critical thinking and logical analysis, and accept whatever pablum that is served as a substitute.

Are Florida's leaders proud of the state's primary involvement in the January 6 tragedy? We haven't heard any speeches from them expressing sadness or regret. I doubt we will. If they stay silent, and the public doesn't read or hear about it, these officials have the masses precisely where they want them: dumb and happy.

The anger and bitterness of that day remains alive and well in Washington today as House Republicans wage holy war over who will be in charge of the party, and what they will do once they have control.

Kevin McCarthy wants to be speaker so badly he sold his soul and conscience to the few most extreme members of the party. He is accused of lacking leadership skills—which is precisely what the rabid 20 who oppose him don't want. They don't want a leader; they want to stoke chaos in the form of revenge politics. For them, to hell with programs that help Americans; it's all about their belief system that is at variance with the principles of Democracy. McCarthy's concession now have more moderates up in arms, with no solution in sight.

Abraham Lincoln said "if you want to test a man's character, give him power." We are seeing the character of these men and women. The core question is what will be done about it?

Meanwhile, the investigation into January 6 continues, not in the House, but in the Department of Justice and in some states. The arc of history bends toward justice.

THE DANGER OF SANCTIMONIOUSNESS

Donald Trump has called Florida Gov. Ron DeSantis sanctimonious. Actually, Trump, in his inimical style, referred to DeSantis as 'Ron De-Sanctimonious.' Whether

Trump himself knows what the word means is beside the point; he message is clear to those who do.

Sanctimonious means someone who's self-righteous; having a holier-than-thou attitude of moral superiority derived from a sense that one's beliefs, actions, or affiliations are of greater virtue than those of the average person. Such a person is arrogant and thinks they are better or more important than other people, and behaves in a way that is rude and too confident.

Trump is right; however, he's also described his own mindset and behavior to a T.

The problem with these self-righteous people is that they unalterably believe they are right and those who disagree with them are wrong. There are no shades of grey here. They won't negotiate; they are rigid in thought; and those who differ with them are the enemy.

The most recent evidence of this is the just-concluded brouhaha over the selection of the Republican speaker of the House. The extreme right represented by Matt Gaetz, Lauren Boebert, Chip Roy and a few others held Kevin McCarthy hostage until they won concessions that will affect the flow of the people's business in Congress. But of course, that is of no concern to them; for this small group, power is everything and they didn't want that power residing in the speaker's hands. For McCarthy, realizing his lifelong dream of being speaker trumped everything else. To accomplish his goal, he handed on a silver platter whatever sense of honor and conscience he had to these extremist House members.

To be sure, there are other House Republicans who will benefit from this, and many of them are just as sanctimonious and extreme as Trump, DeSantis and their ilk. Remember, 139 Republican House members joined with eight senators in voting to overturn the 2020 presidential election based solely on a lie without a shred of evidence in their hands. Those numbers represent 32 percent of the House and 27 percent of the entire Congress! This was no small, isolated group of legislative outcasts!

Many of those 147 remain in Congress today, and some new House members just as sanctimonious as their haughty colleagues joined Congress just the other day.

While hundreds have been jailed over January 6, not a single elected official who was involved in the leadup to January 6, the events of that day, and the aftermath have been held accountable for their acts. In fact, some current elected officials have done everything they can to prevent the scofflaws from being held accountable even as they seek accountability from their "enemies."

The mentality that drove January 6 is still with us. While we may be assured that our Democracy held, we must not become so confident that we delude ourselves into believing it can't happen again. A smarter, more appealing leader may well succeed where another failed.

THE GOAL OF THE REPUBLICAN PARTY IS TO DESTROY LIBERALISM OF THE 1930s AND BEYOND, AND REPLACE IT WITH RIGHT-WING IDEOLOGY

(This is a Facebook discussion involving two well-versed individuals and me. It started over a post that discusses what Florida Governor Ron DeSantis has done to destroy liberalism in Florida through restrictive voting laws; gerrymandering of legislative districts; suppressing academic freedom by removing subjects that might cause psychological discomfort; discriminating against certain groups such as the LGBTQ+ communities; etc., all in the name of freedom. His statement that liberalism is an ideology that must be replaced by conservative thought, led to the following posts.)

GW: If liberalism is an ideology, so is conservatism. DeSantis appears to be choosing one ideology over the other by effectively diminishing liberal thought and replacing it with conservative thought. Academic freedom involves teaching both schools of thought--along with others-- allowing for inquiry and debate. This is how students learn to think critically and reason logically. Teaching the blind acceptance of an ideology is indoctrination. DeSantis certainly doesn't want that, does he?

WC: Actually, liberalism is a personality disorder like smoking or alcoholism, which can be recovered from by admitting there's a problem. DeSantis has exploited the silly excesses on many campuses today. For instance, Stanford's recent list of unacceptable words.

GW: If conservatism is the cure, we're in a deep dive.

DS: History is repeating itself again. Hitler did the same thing and forced his ideology into Germany's public education system in the 1930s.

GW: I agree that liberalism has its silly moments, but nothing compares to the craziness that passes for conservatism today. I also agree that history repeats itself, and we are in the midst of a lesson being repeated.

WC: I reject Hitler analogies. When Hitler came to power, Germany had just lost a world war. It was saddled with crippling reparation payments. There was a worldwide depression. Europe had a thousand-year history of antisemitism. To accept similarities to the 1920s and 30s, you have to disregard all the dissimilarities in conditions today.

GW: There certainly are differences, but there are ideological similarities–discontent with the nation's drift, resentment of government, anger at the status quo, scapegoating for the nation's ills, the rise of the demagogue feeding discontent and fueling anger, etc. I wouldn't dismiss Germany out of hand; there are lessons to be learned.

WC: But those similarities are of far less magnitude. About 100 years ago, people were less educated and less sophisticated, more tribal. Communication was primitive, although today it's easily abused (esp. social media). But demagogues are more easily exposed and ridiculed today.

GW: Of course times were different, but human nature doesn't change. Certainly people were less educated back then, but there is a difference between education and learning. People may receive a good education in math, science and technology, but learn very little about human nature and the human experience. As for exposing demagogues, it took a near coup to expose a demagogue, but there are others on the horizon far more polished and appealing than the last one–who still carries some weight despite everything we've learned about him.

WC: Human nature doesn't change, in that haters will always hate, but they don't win any more. It wasn't a near coup on Jan. 6 but an ugly and criminal riot. The morons disrupted the government for a few hours but came nowhere near overthrowing it.

GW: That isn't the conclusion of the House Select Committee. All that was necessary was for a handful of cronies to go along, and the result could well have been far different. Sure, the crazies have always been among us, but until they had a leader who gave them aid and comfort, along with an air of legitimacy, we really had no idea of the size of the hate. There are tens of millions hard core right wingers who support Trump. That number jumps significantly for someone more palatable. We. can remember the days when both parties had liberal, moderate and conservative members. Those days are gone. What I'm saying is that we dismiss the lessons of the 1930s with an "it can't happen here" belief at our peril. Think of today's Republican Party in charge of the legislative and executive branches of the federal government. That doesn't give me a warm, comfortable feeling. Those morons you mention number into the hundreds in Congress. Whatever moderates there are in the Republican Party today would have been considered extreme years ago because so many in the party have moved so much further to the right. Sure, history shows that lunatics lose, but at what cost? Stalin, Hitler and Mussolini cost tens of millions of lives. Mad men exist today, men who would sacrifice many lives for power.

WC: Then what is indicated by the defeat of Trump (and his continued decline since then). There were many reasons for 2016, including a poorly run campaign by HRC -- who still got more votes than he did.

DS: On the other hand, just look at all the millions of people who did vote for him in 2016 and 2020. Most were the blue collars and from the rural areas in the US. Remember, we are an evenly divided country where one half couldn't care less that most of the media labeled Trump a Buffoon. This large block of voters could easily put another wannabe dictator into the White House. Until our country addresses the inequalities that exist in our society and give all American workers a decent way to support themselves — especially those who were left behind (and mostly ignored by both parties) because their once high paying industrial jobs were shipped overseas so the millionaires could become billionaires, this threat to our Democracy will remain. Ironically, if we lose our democracy, the billionaires will ultimately lose the most when the rule of law vanishes because our rule of law currently protects their assets.

WC: You're sadly right that the country is evenly divided and I wish the Trump forces didn't finish such a close second. But I think the MAGA number is declining, sure hope so. I blame the media on both sides; too many people choose MSNBC or Fox & talk radio, and just marinate in a daily discussion that reinforces what they already believe. The media make a lot of money and the listeners think they're well-informed.

GW: We're in a cat-out-of-the-bag situation with the extreme right wing. Just as you can't put the toothpaste back in the tube, I don't think we'll ever get them back in the bottle again, so to speak. We can do everything we can to isolate them or render them outcasts, but I don't think they'll ever just go away. The Democratic Party needs to do some serious soul-searching as well to deal with this broad discontent; but the party will need some level of support from Republicans so that the public sees a bipartisan consensus. The nation stands to suffer if we continue down the current path; the status quo isn't going to get us where we need to be. We need an infusion of conscience and compassion. It would help if more Republicans reject extremism and violence, but that's not happening. How this infusion is accomplished is why we have a government in the first place.

DS: Yes, the MAGA beast can easily be awakened again because the core economic problems that put Trump into office still remains. Although Biden has recognized and tried to address these problems in his first two years in office but will now likely come to an end with Republicans controlling the House.

GW: I recall several commentary that we are two elections away from disaster. This was before the 2020 cycle, which didn't turn out as bad as expected for Democrats. But that was largely due to the foul-ups by the Republicans. And now they have the House--if they can keep it. In 2024, if they keep the House, gain the Senate (which is probable) and the White House, they'll be able to pass whatever they want, and have it signed into law. There is a reason behind Biden and Schumer wanting to fill as many federal judicial vacancies as possible between now and 2025. If the Republicans transform the rest of the judiciary as they have the Supreme Court, where will the disaffected go for justice? And as for the presidential run, a young, vibrant, Republican candidate wrapping freedom around every draconian promise, facing an 82-year-old policy wonk gives me great pause. There are Democrats out there who are young, vibrant and can articulate a message that resonates with the vast majority. Govs. Gretchen Whitmer, J. K. Pritzker and Gavin Newsome come to mind.

THE PATH FORWARD: DARKNESS OR ENLIGHTENMENT?

Immediately after being elected speaker of the House, Kevin McCarthy gave his acceptance speech, followed by the acceptance speech of the minority leader Hakeem Jeffries.

The differences between the two major political parties could not be more profound. The party leaders set out the path they believe the country must take. One offers a path of darkness, the other one of enlightenment.

Here's what they offer.

At the outset, McCarthy effusively praised ex-president Donald Trump for his support and continued influence over the Republican Party. That Trump resorted to multiple lies and violence to remain in office illegally and stole confidential government records is of no concern to him. Trump helped McCarthy realize his lifelong dream, and that's all that really matters.

That McCarthy sold his soul to achieve his goal is evident by what Matt Gaetz, one of the more ardent House extremists, said: "He will have to live the entirety of his speakership in a straitjacket constructed by the rules that we're working on now." Gaetz later explained away his willingness to accept McCarthy after vowing never to support him by saying "I ran out of things I could even imagine to ask for." Such is the strength of the House leader.

McCarthy promised to deregulate business, enhance use of fossil fuels, further restrict immigration, end what he calls "woke indoctrination" in public schools and universities, and eliminate new IRS agents to enforce the nation's tax laws.

Let's look at each promise. First, he wants to deregulate business. Sort of like it was during the 1920s before the nation's economy crashed and burned—until the New Deal of the 1930s eventually led to the nation's rescue, aided by a war that caused conservative isolationists to abandon appeasing Hitler and dissolving the America First group.

Conservatives, however, never liked all those "socialist" government programs that helped the nation eventually survive the Great Depression and even benefitted them. Now, conservatives want to take us back to those "good old days" of unregulated government. Didn't work out well then, won't work out well today. And if businesses try to cheat on their taxes, they won't have to worry about those new 87,000 IRS agents catching their cheating ways. As a former president said in the 1920s, "the business of government is business." Ah, don't conservatives miss the glory days of Calvin Coolidge!!

As for enhanced use of fossil fuels, has anyone noticed the weather extremes over the past several years? Violent storms, raging fires, frigid weather? But for conservatives, there's no such thing as global warming. Well, now they say, maybe there is. But they say we need more energy, and we're not going to shy away from fossil fuels no matter how they affect our climate and environment. And by the way, those horrible forest fires in California are really the result of laser beams anyway, according to that brilliant intellectual Margorie Taylor Greene. Conservatives know so much more than those pesky scientists. Besides, they have their own scientists peddling the junk conservatives like to hear.

Conservatives will restrict immigration to keep those foreigners out of our country. It doesn't matter whether we're all products of immigration; it doesn't matter if immigrants played a decisive role in building our nation, enough is enough. Besides, most of the migrants today are coming from the south, and they already have countries where they come from. Let them live there. America doesn't need them here. And conservatives don't care what the Statue of Liberty says. America must be only for true Americans—those who are here because their ancestors came here seeking freedom from fear, famine and oppression. Anyone who believes otherwise demonstrates "woke" thinking, and we can't have that anymore.

Along that "woke" line, conservatives believe Democracy and freedom have historically been misunderstood. They can't have Americans believing that complete freedom of thought, speech and action are signs of a nation's strength. They can't have people taught from their early years about events that cause psychological discomfort or pain. No, students must be taught things that make them happy, including how exceptional and peaceful we are and have always been. Teaching young minds about the way people treated people throughout history makes them sad, uncomfortable and unhappy. Conservatives must have happy people.

Conservatives can't have our young learn about the Civil War; the teachings of Hitler, Stalin, Mussolini and Mao; economic depressions or war, or anything else that detracts from the state of contentment and joy. Those things that actually make people think and question are called "woke," and just like some governors are eliminating all of those "woke" studies and thought, McCarthy and his conservative cronies vow to take this attack on academic freedom nationwide. More books will be banned; more classes will be removed from the schools. Current class curriculum will be cleansed and sanitized to eliminate hurtful thoughts. Conservatives know what makes people happy, so they will tell everyone what to think, learn and say, and only when that's accomplished will there be true freedom in America.

Some say the opposite of "woke" is ignorance. Conservatives disagree and that's all that matters. They know what is true and that's what they will teach our nation's students. Besides, history teachers are like those pesky scientists with their fancy degrees and other credentials. Conservatives know better because they believe they know better.

Those who disagree will have to be re-educated, or punished for their evil ways.

Fortunately, whatever passes out of the House that purports to accomplish these goals will die in the Senate or by President Biden's veto pen. Still, this is the path conservatives plan to take the country.

Contrast that with what House minority leader Hakeem Jeffries said.

In response to McCarthy's fawning over Trump, Jeffries said "we believe in a country with the peaceful transfer of power." …

"We believe that in America our diversity is a strength—it is not a weakness—an economic strength, a competitive strength, a cultural strength…. We are a gorgeous mosaic of people from throughout the world. As John Lewis would sometimes remind us on this floor, we may have come over on different ships but we're all in the same boat now. We are white. We are Black. We are Latino. We are Asian. We are Native American.

"We are Christian. We are Jewish. We are Muslim. We are Hindu. We are religious. We are secular. We are gay. We are straight. We are young. We are older. We are women. We are men. We are citizens. We are dreamers.

"Out of many, we are one. That's what makes America a great country, and no matter what kind of haters are trying to divide us, we're not going to let anyone take that away from us, not now, not ever. This is the United States of America...

"So on this first day, let us commit to the American dream, a dream that promises that if you work hard and play by the rules, you should be able to provide a comfortable living for yourself and for your family, educate your children, purchase a home, and one day retire with grace and dignity."

In a direct answer to the question of which direction the Congress will choose to take America, Jeffries told his colleagues and the American public the Democrats offer their hand to Republicans to find common ground, but "we will never compromise our principles. House Democrats will always put American values over autocracy...

Then, in a stirring summarization, he said Democrats choose "benevolence over bigotry, the Constitution over the cult, democracy over demagogues, economic opportunity over extremism, freedom over fascism, governing over gaslighting, hopefulness over hatred, inclusion over isolation, justice over judicial overreach, knowledge over kangaroo courts, liberty over limitation, maturity over Mar-a-Lago, normalcy over negativity, opportunity over obstruction, people over politics, quality of life issues over QAnon, reason over racism, substance over slander, triumph over tyranny, understanding over ugliness, voting rights over voter suppression, working families over the well-connected, xenial over xenophobia, 'yes, we can' over 'you can't do it,' and zealous representation over zero-sum confrontation. We will always do the right thing by the American people."

The contrast between the two parties could not be more directly, forcefully or graphically stated. Choose your path.

THE JANUARY 6 COMMITTEE REPORT

I just finished reading the report of the January 6 House committee. There are several versions available; I chose the one published by Celadon Books with the New Yorker because it's an easier version to read. The content is the same; the print size and layout appear somewhat different among the several versions.

The Report is 784 pages, which includes a preface (32 pages); three forwards by the former Speaker of the House Nancy Pelosi, Committee Chair Bennie Thompson and Vice-Chair Liz Cheney; a table of contents; and concludes with 11 recommendations and an epilogue (eight pages).

The Report is divided into an Executive Summary followed by eight separate chapters, with the summary and each chapter followed by endnotes. An endnote is a citation to a particular source that supports a reference in the report itself, or provides a brief explanatory comment placed at the end of a report and arranged sequentially in relation to where the reference appears in the report.

The Executive Summary is 134 pages; the eight chapters total 377 pages.

What is most glaring is the total number of endnotes. The January 6 Report contains a total of 3532 endnotes. The Report is exhaustive, to say the least. Each asserted fact is abundantly supported by endnotes.

The Report lists the names each witness who testified during the committee's televised hearings. A total of 59 witnesses are Republicans; only one witness is a Democrat--an elections official from Michigan. Six witnesses participated in the attack on the capital; several others are law enforcement authorities who were attacked on that dark day.

The Report begins with an Executive Summary of 134 pages followed by 762 endnotes laying out in some detail the anatomy of what transpired leading up to, during, and after January 6.

The eight chapters, each of which goes into exacting detail laying out facts and evidence, are as follows: Ch. 1--"The Big Lie" (39 pages, 317 endnotes);

Ch. 2— "I Just Want to Find 11,780 Votes" (44 pages, 378 endnotes);

Ch. 3— "Fake Electors and the "The President of the Senate Strategy" (19 pages, 141 endnotes);

Ch. 4— "Just Call it Corrupt and Leave the Rest to Me" (31 pages, 329 endnotes);

Ch. 5— "A Coup in Search of a Legal Theory" (43 pages, 329 endnotes);

Ch. 6— "Be There, It Will Be Wild" (42 pages, 502 endnotes);

Ch. 7— "187 Minutes of Dereliction" (36 pages, 341 endnotes); and

Ch. 8— "Analysis of the Attack" (33 pages, 333 endnotes).

For the lawyers out there, this Report reads like an indictment, laying out in great precision the facts, the supporting testimony and evidence, and applying the facts and evidence to the law. The result shows in precise manner how the law was violated on multiple grounds.

At the very least, the Executive Summary should be read by every American who values our nation's history and our form of government.

The Report will be read by reputable historians; many government officials, judges and lawyers; many students of history and government; and others who just want to be informed citizens.

It will not be read by Donald Trump; his diehard loyalists; the MAGAs; those named in the Report as conspirators or co-conspirators including lawyers Rudy Giuliani and John

Eastman; those who sought presidential pardons; those who defied committee subpoenas; the extreme right wing members of Congress; right wing domestic terrorists and extremists such as Roger Stone, Steve Bannon and Alex Jones; QAnon believers; those named in the Report as having committed ethical violations including current members of Congress such as House Speaker Kevin McCarthy and Judiciary Committee Chairman Jim Jordan; those who simply refuse to believe the overwhelming recitation of facts and evidence that is damning to the former president and others; and those who simply don't care.

Those who dismiss the Report as a "witch hunt" or a "hit job," and those who believe Trump, in his own words, "did nothing wrong." are only deluding themselves by buying into his con game. Just ask those who did his bidding on January 6 and who are now behind bars. Just read the testimony of those rioters who testified before the committee. See how regretful they are for believing Trump's Big Lie.

Read the testimony of all those Republicans, including White House staff and even former Trump supporters and appointees who testified uniformly that Trump knew he lost the election but refused to accept it; tried to force an illegal scheme to remain in office illegally; and engaged in a prolonged series of lies that led to violence he could have stopped, but refused to do so. It's all there in black-and-white.

This is a Report for those who want to be informed, and for those future generations to know what happened, and what must be avoided at all costs if this noble experiment in self-government is to survive.

TOWARD A THEOCRATIC JUDICIARY

Here is a preview of coming attractions should Florida Gov. Ron DeSantis (or a like-minded ideologue) ever set foot in the White House as president. Briefly, there was an outspoken anti-abortion trial judge who brought his religion into his judicial decisions. During his campaign last year to remain in office, he made religion a central part of his campaign. He appeared with his wife at several churches saying his opponent, who is Jewish, "needs Jesus. To deny God and to deny the Bible is a person that's — the heart is very hard toward God."

That's it; only those who believe in Jesus believe in God and the Bible. Someone forgot to tell her about the Old Testament, and the existence of other major religions here and around the world. Remember those who believe their religion is superior to all others? Here is an example. For good measure, the judge also added a bit of antisemitism to his campaign.

The voters ousted this judge; obviously he was too much even for the voters of Palm Beach County.

But this judge wasn't out of a job for long. Gov. DeSantis appointed him to the appeals court...a promotion and a reward for making his Christian religion a central core of his judicial writings, and for being a rock-ribbed anti-abortionist.

Bully for him.

DeSantis has convinced millions of voters that only those who are "woke'--defined as those who are aware of and actively attentive to important societal facts and issues--are ideologues. To have him tell it, only conservatives--and extreme conservatives at that--are fair minded, objective thinkers free of ideology. Here is Exhibit A of a rigid ideology, but his supporters believe whatever he says is true and they simply lap it up.

All he needs is to become president and have a compliant senate. Then he can and will fill the federal judiciary with judges whose central core won't be the Constitution and laws, it will be their religious beliefs, dogma and tenets. Our judiciary will become a Christian theology--precisely what our forefathers warned against.

This is what Thomas Jefferson said during his first term as president when he declared his firm belief in the separation of church and state in a letter to the Danbury, Conn. Baptists. He said: "Believing with you that religion is a matter which lies solely between man and his God, that he owes account to none other for his faith or his worship, that the legislative powers of government reach actions only and not opinions, I contemplate with sovereign reverence that act of the whole American people which declared that their legislature should `make no law respecting an establishment of religion, or prohibiting the free exercise thereof,' thus building a wall of separation between church and state."

But those who are more focused on re-writing history to bend it toward their ideology will conveniently forget or ignore the teachings of our forefathers. The ultimate question is whether enough voters will go along for the ride.

THERE IS BLOOD IN THE WATER; TIME FOR THE SHARKS TO ATTACK

Republicans are jumping with joy, doing a collective happy dance, ecstatic over the revelation that fewer than a dozen classified documents from Joe Biden's time as vice president were discovered last fall in a private office.

To them, this is a perfect example of different treatment between Biden and Trump. Forget clear differences, the two situations are the same. Only the foolish and uninformed believe this.

Predictably, Republicans are foaming at the mouth over this unexpected gift now bolstering their planned investigation into the FBI's handling of its raid on Trump's Mar-a-Lago residence.

Republicans are also using this as further evidence that Biden doesn't have the mental capabilities of governing. This, from by and large the same people who believe Trump is a genius and one of the greatest presidents in our nation's history. So much for informed judgment and knowledge of American history.

Republican glee over equating Biden's situation with Trump's again demonstrates the illogic of a false equivalency. There are stark differences between the two, but that doesn't matter to Republicans who want to investigate the investigators instead of investigating Trump and his cohorts for their demonstrated criminal activity and unethical behavior as amply set out in the House January 6 committee report, or for Trump's admitted theft of government classified records and subsequent mishandling of them at his estate.

Let's look at those differences.

First, we don't know who took this small number of government records and put them in a locked closet in Biden's former office. They were found by Biden's attorneys last November as they were vacating office space at the Penn Biden Center in Washington, D.C. Biden periodically used this space from mid-2017 until the start of the 2020 campaign. The use of this office was part of his relationship with the University of Pennsylvania, where he was an honorary professor from 2017 to 2019.

On the day of this discovery, the White House Counsel's Office notified the National Archives, which took possession of the materials the following morning. These documents were not the subject of any previous request or inquiry by the National Archives.

Attorney General Merrick Garland asked the Trump-appointed U.S. attorney in Chicago to investigate the matter.

In sharp contrast, we know exactly who took boxes of classified government records from the White House to his home. Trump has been most vocal about this, ludicrously maintaining that he declassified them "just by thinking about it." The FBI found numerous records strewn about his property, yet Trump continues to claim he "did nothing wrong."

Trump also defied requests to turn over the records once the Archives learned of the theft. He turned over some, but not all. It was only after Trump refused to turn over all records that the FBI was left with no choice but to take possession of those stolen records through the normal process of obtaining a subpoena from a federal judge upon a showing of the lawfully required probable cause, and enforcing that lawful subpoena.

Second, Biden has asked for investigation through the attorney general. Trump never asked for an investigation into how those records wound up in Mar-a-Lago. Of course, one wasn't needed; Trump's crime was committed in broad daylight because, again, he "did nothing wrong." To him, it's perfectly normal to take government records and store them at his home, no matter what the law says about turning records over to the government.

Third, there is the stark difference between the cooperation and the absence of obstruction in which Biden and his lawyers engaged compared to Trump's defiant behavior.

Fourth, Trump's actions took place while he was president; Biden was vice president from 2017 to 2021.

Still, this disclosure has stirred up a hornet's nest at a time when Trump is in facing increasing legal peril. The Republican House majority that has already promised to investigate those who investigated Trump, are now rushing feverishly to undermine those investigations against him and unleash a wave of counter-investigations against Biden.

This disclosure only adds blood to the water for the Republican sharks to attack. One example of this, and how Republicans are working overtime to poison the well, is House Oversight Committee Chairman James Comer's statement: "This is (a) further concern that there is a two-tiered justice system."

The Republican Party will go to extremes to undermine our Democratic institutions, including our system of justice, solely to appease and protect Donald Trump.

TAKE YOUR SOMA; YOU'LL FEEL BETTER, BE DISTRACTED, AND WON'T ASK ANNOYING QUESTIONS

The year is 1932. America is into its third year of the greatest economic crisis in our nation's history. The economy continued to deteriorate following the stock market crash of 1929, leaving one of every four workers unemployed. As stocks continued to fall during the early 1930s, businesses failed. By 1932, Banks failed and life savings were lost, leaving many Americans destitute. With no job and no savings, thousands of Americans lost their homes, forced into living on the streets or in old cars.

In that same year, as Americans faced great suffering, Aldous Huxley published his most important work, "Brave New World," describing life in a dystopian society where there is great suffering or injustice. The author describes mass psychological manipulation and conditioning, focusing on a drug he calls soma.

In this "Brave New World," the government seeks to prevent its people from speaking freely and thinking by giving them soma, a legal drug that is available for them every day. Reviewers noted that the theme here is clear: wouldn't it be easier for government to manipulate its people and to know that there's nothing left in their heads other than rainbows, pink butterflies and unicorns? Would the great leaders of our present world go this far to secure their office, and would there be happier, more peaceful lives for the citizens?

Note the times when this book was written. Huxley, who wrote his work in 1931, was observing regimes such as Nazi Germany and the USSR. He wrote this cautionary tale to warn Americans about how society could become in the near future. And many of the things that he metaphorically warned us about can be seen in modern-day America.

For Huxley, soma is a key symbol: a drug consumed regularly by most, if not all, of the state's citizens to ease temporary pain. The reliance on soma is clearly a metaphor for how people choose to distract themselves with short term pleasures rather than face their problems at hand. We can recall a cultural phenomenon during the 1960s—the answer to all problems is in a pill.

"Brave New World" is often compared with George Orwell's equally dystopian "1984" published in 1949. Each author viewed American society as a place of darkness.

One reviewer describes how each author write from different points of view, yet reach the same depressing conclusions:

"Huxley feared that there would be no reason to ban a book, for there would be no one who wanted to read one. Orwell feared those who would deprive us of information. Huxley feared those who would give us so much that we would be reduced to passivity and egoism. Orwell feared that the truth would be concealed from us. Huxley feared the truth would be drowned in a sea of irrelevance. Orwell feared we would become a captive culture. Huxley feared we would become a trivial culture, preoccupied with some equivalent of the feelies, the orgy porgy, and the centrifugal bumblepuppy.

As Huxley remarked in "Brave New World Revisited," the civil libertarians and rationalists who are ever on the alert to oppose tyranny "failed to take into account man's almost infinite appetite for distractions." In *1984*, Huxley added, people are controlled by inflicting pain. In Brave New World, they are controlled by inflicting pleasure. In short, Orwell feared that what we hate will ruin us. Huxley feared that what we love would ruin us."

Both are novels, considered works of fiction. Yet, neither is describing an imaginary society, but rather offers a political satire of the society he was observing around him at the time.

The relevance of both works should be clear as a bell today. Two recent examples make this abundantly clear.

First, House Republicans continue to ignore Donald Trump's theft and mishandling of hundreds of classified government records, while raging against President Biden despite having no evidence that he took, or knew that the few records were taken by others, to an office in Pennsylvania.

Second, ignoring testimony from former DOJ officials on how Trump tried to "weaponize" the Justice Department to spread false claims about election fraud, House Republicans plan to create a special Judiciary subcommittee on what they call the "weaponization of the federal government," a topic that Republicans have signaled could include reviewing investigations into Trump. Further, they are preparing a wide-ranging investigation into law enforcement and national security agencies, raising the prospect of politically charged fights with the Biden administration over access to sensitive information like highly classified intelligence and the details of continuing criminal inquiries by the Justice Department.

To Republicans, Trump is a victim, maligned by America's mortal enemies. Further, those who aided and abetted him are equally victims. Their good names must be cleansed while the real criminals—those who followed the law in conducting their investigations--are investigated, prosecuted and punished.

To accomplish this Great Distraction, Republicans must, echoing Huxley's words, feed the masses verbal soma that will reduce them to passivity and egoism. This soma will allow truth about Trump and his extremists to be drowned in a sea of irrelevance. They're hoping the masses will become preoccupied with some equivalent of the feelies, the orgy porgy, and the centrifugal bumblepuppy. Republican leaders are keenly aware of, in Huxley's words, "man's almost infinite appetite for distractions." (Re-read this last sentence again.) In Brave New World, people are controlled by inflicting pleasure, largely through soma. In short, take your soma; don't worry, be happy.

When they distract by railing against the Biden administration and the Justice Department for pointing out Trump's criminal conduct and promising to investigate the investigators, Republicans are feeding the masses soma. When they want the public to believe they are the pillars of righteousness, and those who disagree or question them are "enemies of the people" who must be punished, they are feeding soma to the masses.

When they trample on academic freedom, sanitize curriculum to avoid psychological discomfort, control through economic punishment businesses that disagree with them, restrict voting, etc., all in the name of freedom and liberty, Republicans are feeding soma to the masses.

Whether soma is taken for that feel-good feeling of happiness born of distraction from annoying, pesky reality, is up to each person. I'll pass.

JOE BIDEN, GOVERNMENT RECORDS, AND CHAIN OF CUSTODY

A second batch of government records, some of which may be classified, has been found by Joe Biden's lawyers at a second location where he had an office.

While the Justice Department is investigating this latest disclosure, along with the previous one, it's worth remembering what Richard Nixon failed to learn—it's not the crime, it's the cover-up. And then there's that high ethical standard of avoiding even the appearance of any impropriety.

Not to suggest there's a crime here--unlike Donald Trump's situation where he knowingly took hundreds of government records to his home and maintains he did nothing wrong, or any ethical impropriety. However, the longer Biden's situation festers, the worse it looks. And appearances can mean everything.

To get in front of this now, this matter must be fully investigated by an independent authority. The attorney general should either appoint a special counsel, or as in the first records discovery, a united states attorney originally appointed by Donald Trump. My preference is for a special counsel with impeccable credentials. Extraordinary circumstances require extraordinary measures. When the subject is the president of the United States, extraordinary measures are most appropriate.

In cases involving documents such as government confidential records, lawyers are well familiar with the phrase "chain of custody." This is what's involved here. Any investigation must track the movement of these documents from their original location, through collection, safeguarding, and review, to the location when they were found. There must be no gap or unexplainable missing link.

This "chain of custody" search is done by documenting for each step along the chain the identity of each person who handled these records by date and time, together with the purpose for handling, reason for examination and necessity for review from beginning to end. Every step along the chain must be painstakingly accounted for and fully explained. In a court of law, if it can be shown that the chain of custody was broken, then the court can deem the evidence in question potentially tainted and therefore inadmissible. This is why chain of custody is so vital in situations such as this.

The questions that must be answered are that same that are familiar to lawyers as well as journalists: who had possession; what purpose did each person have for possessing them; when were they in possession of each person; where were they in each person's possession; how did each person gain access; and why did each person have access. If there is overlap in the explanation, detail is better than repetition. What is essential is that there be no gaps in this chronology.

And in getting those answers, time is of the essence.

LIES, FRAUD, HYPOCRISY, AND THE CONSTITUTION

Newly minted Republican Rep. George Santos of New York is a liar, fraud and quite possibly a tax cheat who has been asked to resign by Republicans in his home state.

House Speaker Kevin McCarthy, when asked about Santos' resigning over fabrications about his résumé and questions about his finances, said: "I try to stick by the Constitution. The voters elected him to serve."

The voters also elected Joe Biden to serve, but the Constitution didn't stop McCarthy from supporting Donald Trump's repeated election fraud lie. And it didn't stop election denier McCarthy from supporting Trump's effort to stop the constitutional certification of the electoral college votes on January 6.

Seems that McCarthy sticks by the Constitution when it supports his hold on power, but either ignores it or tries to sidestep it when it applies to all things Trump—and with his defense of Santos, anything that allows him to stay in power. He has a narrow House majority and can't afford any peel-offs no matter how egregious Santos' conduct might be. After all, if voters re-elected Matt Gaetz, Lauren Boebert and Marjorie Taylor Greene after all their reported craziness and shenanigans, who's to say the voters in New York won't re-elect Santos. Seems lots of voters aren't concerned with lying, fraud, crazy behavior, etc.

To makes McCarthy's Constitutional stick defense even more laughable, he said if there are ethical concerns about Santos, they will be taken up by the House Ethics Committee—the same committee that has referrals on McCarthy himself and House Judiciary Committee Chairman and fellow ardent Trump loyalist Jim Jordan, for their unethical behavior surrounding January 6. Anyone who believes McCarthy's handpicked ethics committee members will do an unbiased and thorough job investigating Santos, as well as McCarthy and Jordan, had better buy into all that cryptocurrency and become instant millionaires--or perhaps invest in beachfront property in Omaha.

His humorous deference to the Constitution doesn't mask his phoniness or hypocrisy, but he has been handed the "hypocrisy" claim on a silver platter over two instances of confidential classified records found in offices used by Biden during his years as vice president. To him—and the other Trump acolytes who had remained silent about Trump's theft and mishandling of similar records—Biden is a hypocrite for criticizing Trump over stolen documents.

Well, that's fine for their base and provides some fertilizer for their "whataboutism." Factually, however, this reliance is woefully misplaced. Not that facts matter when you have fertilizer to sling and don't care about facts.

First, Trump actually stole records; there is no evidence Biden stole any records.

Second, Trump mishandled hundreds of records, strewing them around his estate. Biden's records, clearly marked, were found in a secure location.

Third, when Trump was initially found out by the National Archives and the NA requested return of all stolen records, he returned some—but not all—of them. His refusal to return hundreds of stolen records is why the FBI was required to seize the records he still possessed by asking a federal judge to issue a search warrant based on probable cause that a crime had been committed. The NA never made any similar request of Biden because his lawyers promptly turned over the records to the NA.

The bottom line is that Trump committed a crime; there is no evidence Biden committed a crime. Still, if the "whataboutism" defense is weak, and it's all they have, they must go with what they have. The base will buy it. Remember the game plan: tell a lie often enough, and it becomes the truth.

While this stew simmers, House Republicans have begun passing legislation that has no chance of becoming law, but because this legislation is red meat for the right wing, it makes for loud and long talking points among the party faithful. They know their bills will die in the Senate or by veto, but passing laws for the public's benefit isn't their plan; it's all about anger, revenge, payback and keeping the base raging at the Democrats. And as long as it works, this is what the Republicans will do. For them, this is better than actually governing.

And then there are those promised investigations, now on overdrive super fueled by the Biden documents revelation.

Although on a different subject, most relevant are these immortal words from famed actress Bette Davis: "Fasten your seatbelts - it's going to be a bumpy night."

NIXON. REAGAN. CLINTON. TRUMP. BIDEN. IT'S NOT THE CRIME; IT'S THE COVER UP

Aside from being president, these five also have something else in common. Each faced scandal, in large part of their own making.

Richard Nixon had Watergate. Ronald Reagan had Iran-Contra. Bill Clinton had Monicagate. Donald Trump had the Big Lie and theft of government records. Joe Biden has discrepancies in reporting disclosures of government records. The first four had scandals that erupted during their time in the White House. Biden's occurred as he was leaving office as vice president in 2017 but has now poured over into his presidency.

Watergate involved attempts to cover up the Nixon administration's involvement in the 1972 break-in of the Democratic National Committee headquarters at the Washington, D.C., Watergate Office Building. Those arrested had cash that was traced to Nixon's re-election committee. Congressional investigative committees held hearings, during which witnesses testified Nixon had approved plans to cover up his administration's involvement in the break-in, and that there was a voice-activated taping system in the Oval Office. These major revelations and Nixon's efforts to obstruct the investigation led to impeachment proceedings. After the Supreme Court ruled that Nixon must turn over the tapes, and upon learning of a lack of support in the senate on conviction, Nixon resigned. The

Watergate scandal gripped the nation for more than two years.

Iran-Contra began shortly after Reagan took office. Between 1981 and 1986, senior administration officials secretly facilitated the sale of arms to Iran, which was the subject of an arms embargo. The administration hoped to use the proceeds of the arms sale to fund the Contras, a right-wing rebel group, in Nicaragua. Further funding of the Contras by the government had been prohibited by Congress; thus, this scheme violated federal law. Several Reagan administration officials were indicted for their involvement, including the secretary of defense, national security advisor, assistant secretary of state, and CIA officials. No official served prison time, as they eventually received pardons from Reagan's successor, George H.W. Bush. While investigating committees found no evidence that Reagan himself knew of the extent of this operation, Reagan, who was past 70 at the time, suffered from the perception of being out of touch because of his age.

Monicagate was the shorthand description—harking to Watergate—of the Clinton–Lewinsky sex scandal involving then-president Clinton and Monica Lewinsky, a White House intern. Their sexual relationship began in 1995—when Clinton was 49 years old and Lewinsky was 22 years old—and lasted 18 months, ending in 1997. Clinton ended a televised speech in late January 1998 with the later infamous statement: "I did not have sexual relations with that woman, Ms. Lewinsky." Further investigation led to charges of perjury and to the impeachment of Clinton in 1998 by the House of Representatives. He was subsequently acquitted on all impeachment charges of perjury and obstruction of justice in a 21-day U.S. Senate trial.

Trump's catchphrase is the Big Lie. Having lost his 2020 bid for re-election he, along with a few cronies, concocted a scheme that involved repeatedly lying about a "rigged" election, stoking violence among his most extreme supporters, ultimately leading to the January 6 attack on the nation's capital causing multiple deaths and property destruction, all designed to prevent lawful certification of Joe Biden's election as president. Compounding the several crimes uncovered by House committee investigators and set out in their comprehensive report, Trump was further found to have stolen government records from the White House and later mishandled them at his estate.

Biden's situation involving government records located in a former office and residence is under investigation. It hasn't reached the level of a scandal yet, but it could, depending on the answer to that classic question asked by Sen. Howard Baker during the Watergate investigation of 50 years ago: "What did the president know and when did he know it?"

Nixon knew of the break-in crime and participated in its cover-up. Reagan didn't have personal knowledge of the illegal sale of arms but nevertheless suffered the scandal on his presidency of being perceived as the out-of-touch.

Clinton believed he could finagle his way out of a scandal he created.

For Nixon and Clinton, the cover up was their undoing. Both believed they could get away with it. After all, they were the most powerful men on the planet. They learned the hard way that it's not about the crime, it's the cover up. Had Nixon fessed up early on and even concocted a story about concern for national security; had Clinton fessed up and showed remorse and contrition, both more than likely would have avoided impeachment.

Reagan's place in history as a popular president is assured, although there is that notation that says Iran-Contra took place during his years in the White House.

Trump has taken a completely different approach. Rather than trying to cover up his conduct, he's been up front and confrontational about it. This, of course, started when he called his telephone conversation with Ukraine's president seeking dirt on Joe Biden's son in exchange for releasing congressionally approved funds "perfect." He blasted the ensuing impeachment as a "witch hunt." Despite dozens of his own staffers testifying that Trump knew he lost the election, he continues to double down on his Big Lie, and millions—including members of Congress—continue to believe him and show unfailing deference toward him. Finally, for his records theft, he insists he "did nothing wrong." Rather than try to distract or fend off the evidence of wrongdoings, he's taken a "so what?" defiant attitude, thumbing his nose at anyone who disagrees with him.

Thus far, Biden has cooperated with investigators; yet, there are some inconsistent responses by his aides and unanswered questions regarding the timeline—why he waited so long to disclose what was discovered a couple of months ago. Certainly a legitimate question that deserves clear answers. Hindsight is certainly 20-20, but it would seem that immediate public disclosure would have been a better stance to take.

The lesson learned from Nixon and Clinton is that the cover-up is often worse than the crime. Will the ultimate outcome of the Biden investigation place him in the Reagan mode of lack of personal knowledge, with age a factor? Or will he wind up in the Nixon-Clinton mode of unsuccessfully trying to cover up what he knew, and when he knew it?

Stay tuned.

A DELICATE BALANCE

That religion plays a vital role in America is without question. In fact, religion lies at the heart of nations; very existence around the globe. Just visit the Vatican in Rome, Notre Dame in Paris, Westminster Abbey in London, the Blue Mosque and Hagia Sophia in Istanbul, etc. and see firsthand these magnificent buildings that are dedicated to the overwhelming power of faith.

It seems that every term of the Supreme Court has another hot-button case before it that tests how Americans are to accommodate religion along with their daily lives. Our forefathers frequently referred to the separation of church and state, yet the precise meaning of this phrase waxes and wanes, depending upon the Court's composition and the mood of the public. Both, however, are not always in sync.

In recent years, the Court has considered a case in which a baker refused to prepare a cake for a gay couple, claiming that to do so was against one's Christian beliefs opposing gay marriage. There is also the case of a football coach who was told he, along with several players joining him, couldn't pray on the field after each game.

The baker maintained she was exercising creative expression in making a wedding cake, and shouldn't be forced to act against her well-founded religious beliefs in doing so.

The football coach said he was privately exercising his religious beliefs in silently praying after the game, and that the players who chose to join him were acting of their own free will, and not under coercion on the coach's part.

The Court ultimately supported the baker and coach.

It seems that so long as there is no coercion to violate one's religious beliefs, and no force requiring prayer against one's will, religious exercises will be accommodated.

It is a delicate balance.

The Supreme Court has agreed to hear the case of an evangelical Christian mail carrier who says the U.S. Postal Service should have granted his request that he be spared Sunday shifts based on his religious belief that it is a day of worship and rest. This employment discrimination claim could force employers to do more to accommodate the religious practices of their workers.

At the core of this case is an effort to make it easier for employees to bring religious claims under Title VII of the Civil Right Act, which prohibits workplace discrimination of various forms, including based on religion.

The accommodation here is between Sunday shifts and religious beliefs that Sunday is a day of worship and rest. Judging from the baker's and coach's cases, it seems consistent that the Court will side with the mail carrier. The postal service, as the second largest employer in the United States with over 500,000 employees, could relatively easily accommodate for the Sunday shift while providing service on that particular day.

Courts like to decide cases as narrowly as possible, even though judges and lawyers thrive on changing the facts of a case and asking whether the outcome would be the same. This happens in law school every day.

In the baker's case, the overriding question is whether the outcome would have been the same if the baker, knowing a person is gay, refused to sell that person a bag of donuts or a cake on display for ready purchase. In short, could a business owner, citing religious beliefs, flatly refuse to provide service to a person whose lifestyle conflicts with the owner's beliefs? What about a restaurant waiter who knows the customer's lifestyle or religious views are contrary to the waiter's? Could the waiter refuse service based on that knowledge?

In the coach's case, could he refuse to play a player who refuses to pray with him? What about the religious beliefs of those players who aren't Christian? If a player claims he wasn't put in the game because he refused to pray, how would the player actually prove that in court? Suppose the coach decided to pray audibly; would that change the outcome?

As for the mail carrier, suppose he sees, among the letters and packages he must deliver, an item addressed to Planned Parenthood, or a return address from a known abortion clinic or doctor. Can the carrier legitimately refuse to deliver on the grounds that to do so would compel him to violate his Christian beliefs?

There is a well-known saying among judges and lawyers that "hard cases make bad law," meaning that an extreme case is a poor basis for a general rule that would cover a wider range of less extreme cases. Yet, this familiar phrase has long been turned upside down as well, as cases that are – by and large – not too difficult may lead to results that are more along the line of "be careful what you wish for."

This upside down version seems to be in play here. Whether it be a baker forced to make a cake against his religious beliefs, telling a football coach he can't silently pray after a game, or a mail carrier having to work on Sunday against his religious beliefs, the ultimately question is about those circumstances that are demonstrably more profound and pervasive, such as those I mention above.

A delicate balance indeed.

MORE REVELATIONS OF RECORDS FOUND ON JOE BIDEN'S PROPERTY: HE NEEDS TO STOP THE BLEEDING

To analogize a phrase from war ("death by a thousand cuts"), this is an example of a political disaster by a thousand cuts. Each revelation about classified records being found on Joe Biden's property, which is met by silence, only inflicts further cuts.

Whatever Biden knows, he needs to tell the American people now. He can't wait until the investigation is complete; each revelation may invoke an additional time-impacted inquiry, and time isn't on his side. In short, this can't be allowed to drag out.

Records are either deliberately, negligently or inadvertently taken. That's what the facts will disclose. But Biden's silence only fuels speculation, and the last thing he needs going into the second half of his first term is to have speculation run amok.

His supporters are frustrated because of the silence and reports of staff inconsistencies. Republicans have their political knives out ready to make his life a complete misery, and dash any hopes of passing legislation.

A president's power to get things done is tied directly to his ability to command public favor. A strong president will use the bully pulpit of the office to get things done. A president viewed as weak will accomplish nothing.

Whatever the truth is, it's best to hear it from Biden now, than from his lawyers or staff members, or from a special counsel, later when it may be too late.

THE FILIBUSTER: A HISTORY

The filibuster. This legislative tool, available only in the United States Senate, is defined as a parliamentary procedure to prevent a measure from being brought to a vote. The most common form of filibuster occurs when one or more senators attempt to delay or block a vote on a bill by extending debate on the measure. Politicians have used filibustering since Sen. John Calhoun created the concept in 1841. It is provided for in the Senate rules.

The notion that majority rules does not necessarily apply to the Senate; some actions require 60 votes. With its current makeup, the chances of getting 60 Senate votes to do anything meaningful, except perhaps to adjourn, is remote at best.

The filibuster is either a means of preventing bad legislation from becoming law, or of obstructing needed legislation for the public good, depending on whose ox is being gored. The rule has certain limitations and exceptions which can be altered by the Senate, but change is subject to the filibuster. The rule also provides for ending a filibuster, called cloture.

In its original form, invoking the filibuster required the senator to "take to the floor" and speak against the pending legislation; however, currently, this is no longer required. Today, senators can merely signal their intent to object, even privately, and that's enough for Senate leaders to take action. Leaders sometimes just drop the issue from floor consideration. At other times, they push ahead, taking cumbersome steps to cut off the filibuster and move forward with the proceedings.

Although its claimed purpose is to "extend debate," in practice, it's a stalling tactic. Here are five famous filibusters in U.S. history:

Jefferson Smith (James Stewart), 1939
Film's full runtime: 2 hours, 11 minutes

Sen. Jefferson Smith (played by James Stewart, the star of *Mr. Smith Goes to Washington*) filibusters a bill that will permit dam construction on the site of his proposed boys' camp; the filibuster succeeds when Sen. Harrison Paine (Claude Rains) confesses to his role in a graft scheme and tries to shoot himself.

Rand Paul, 2013
Filibuster length: 13 hours

Sen. Rand Paul, R-Ky., revived the tradition of talking filibusters, protesting U.S. drone policy by blocking a vote on CIA Director John Brennan and holding the floor for just under 13 hours. Brennan eventually won confirmation.

Huey P. Long, 1935
Filibuster length: 15 hours, 30 minutes

Sen. Huey P. Long spent 15 hours and 30 minutes arguing against passage of a New Deal bill that would have given jobs to political enemies in Louisiana. The flamboyant Long peppered his filibuster with readings of the Constitution, Shakespeare plays and oyster recipes.

Wayne Morse, 1953
Filibuster length: 22 hours, 26 minutes

Sen. Wayne Morse, an independent from Oregon, set a longevity record in filibustering over tidelands oil legislation.

Strom Thurmond, 1957
Filibuster length: 24 hours, 18 minutes

Sen. Strom Thurmond, R-S.C., broke Morse's record with an unsuccessful filibuster against the Civil Rights Act of 1957. Thurmond, subsisting on throat lozenges, malted milk tablets and a steak sandwich, spoke 24 hours and 18 minutes before concluding with the line, "I expect to vote against the bill." During his time "on the floor," Thurmond asserted that the civil rights bill was unconstitutional and constituted "cruel and unusual punishment". He went on to read documents primarily related to the United States and its history, including the Declaration of Independence, the election laws of each state in alphabetical order, a U.S. Supreme Court ruling, the U.S. Bill of Rights, and George Washington's Farewell Address. Consuming 84 pages in the Congressional Record, the filibuster cost taxpayers over $6,000 in printing costs.

In 2013, Sen. Ted Cruz, R-Texas, vowed to speak on the Senate floor "until I am no longer able to stand" in opposition to President Obama's health care law.

As can be readily seen, there is nothing that prevents a senator from reading the Manhattan telephone book, Aesop's Fables, or anything else for that matter, during his/her filibuster. A filibustering senator should wear comfortable shoes, have friendly colleagues prepared to ask questions or provide comments, and have a strong bladder. According to Senate rule, no bathroom breaks are permitted (although this can be tinkered with by careful use of one's friends).

Current debate involves either ending the filibuster completely or returning this tool to its original format of "taking the floor."

For reasons that should be self-evident, Democrats have floated the idea of complete elimination; however, at least two Democrat senators say they oppose this, causing President Biden to favor returning the filibuster to its original form. For their part, the Republicans have vowed a "scorched earth" effort to block any change.

The Democrats fear that if they make a change, it will backfire if or when the Republicans once again gain control of the Senate. Some Democrats ask whether they really believe a Republican majority won't do whatever they want regardless of what the Democrats do with their current slim majority.

So, what we have at this point is another Senate stalemate on whether to change the rule the results in a stalemate on legislation.

SOME REPUBLICANS BELIEVE TODAY'S REPUBLICAN PARTY IS THE PARTY OF LINCOLN. THEY'RE WRONG

Republican Party leaders often refer to their party as "The Party of Lincoln." At one time, this was true; however, this assertion overlooks our nation's history of political party realignment. Today's Republican Party is certainly NOT "The Party of Lincoln."

During debate on the 1964 Civil Rights Act, Democrat Sen. Robert Byrd of West Virginia took to the floor and filibustered this legislation for 14 hours and 13 minutes. Upon signing this act into law, President Lyndon Johnson is reported to have said "There goes the South (to the Republicans) for a generation." At that time, the south was run by Southern Democrats who very much opposed civil rights. Whether LBJ said this or not, it is prophetic, and it has lasted for generations up to the present.

(As an aside, Republican Senate Minority Leader Mitch McConnell recently said the Senate filibuster has no connection to race. He either forgets or ignores Sen Byrd's 1964 filibuster, or the 24-hour-18-minute filibuster by South Carolina Sen. Strom Thurmond in opposition to the 1957 Civil Rights Act. During his time "on the floor," Thurmond asserted that the civil rights bill was unconstitutional and constituted "cruel and unusual punishment.")

As you can see from the brief online discussion below, political party realigning is very much a part of our nation's history. Here is that history.

A party realignment occurs when the country transitions from being mostly run by one political party to mostly run by another political party. During party realignments, some groups of people who used to vote for one party vote for the other one. Sometimes, political parties end and new ones begin. Party realignments can happen because of important events in history or because of changes in the kinds of people in the country.

1820s

In the early 1800s, America had the "First Party System" with the Federalist Party and the Democratic-Republican Party. When James Monroe was elected President of the United States, the Federalists died out. There was an "Era of Good Feelings" of one-party rule by the Democratic-Republicans. In the United States presidential election, 1824, four different men ran for President, all as Democratic-Republicans. John Quincy Adams was elected.

After the election, Andrew Jackson formed a new party called the Democrats. Jackson's party was strongest in the South and West, and in some cities (at this time, only a few Americans lived in cities). Soon after Jackson's election, another party formed around supporters of Adams and Henry Clay. It was first called the National Republican

Party, and later the Whig Party. The Whigs were strong in the North, and among the middle class and businessmen. The system of Democrats and Whigs is called the "Second Party System."

1850s-60s

After the Kansas-Nebraska Act, the "Second Party System" ended:

- Whigs and Democrats who did not want to pass the Kansas-Nebraska Act, as well as Free- HYPERLINK "https://simple.wikipedia.org/wiki/Free_Soil_Party" Soilers, formed a new party called the Republicans. The Republicans' main goal was stopping slavery, but they also liked many of the things the Whigs liked.
- The Whig Party broke up. Some Whigs joined the Know-Nothing Party or other small parties for the 1856 election. More joined the Republicans or Democrats.
- In the 1860 election, Know-Nothings and Southern Democrats who supported the Union formed the Constitutional Union Party. During and after the American Civil War, the Know-Nothings and Unionists were part of the Republican Party.

- In 1860, what was left of the Democratic Party broke into Northern and Southern wings, one on each side of the Civil War.
- By 1868, the Democratic Party came back together and there was the "Third Party System" of Democrats and Republicans.

1930s

America went from being mostly Republican in the 1920s to mostly Democratic in the 1930s. This was due to America becoming much more urban, and the Great Depression. Franklin D. Roosevelt formed a coalition that would mostly last until 1964 called the "New Deal coalition."

- Urban areas became very Democratic. They voted very heavily for people like Al Smith and Roosevelt. They had been growing rapidly, due in part to immigrants who were part of democratic political machines.
- African American citizens had been moving from the South into large Northern cities, in large part due to racial segregation. Before the 1930s, they had either not voted or voted Republican. Under Roosevelt, they mostly voted Democratic.

- Roosevelt also made gains in every part of the country, due to his mass appeal and the desire to end the depression.
- For the first time in its history, the Democrats were a statist party instead of a libertarian one.

1960s-80s

In the 1960s and 70s, the New Deal coalition fell apart. This was due to the Civil Rights Movement, Roe v. Wade, Vietnam War and the suburbanization of America. What changed:

- After the 1964 Civil Rights Act, many white, conservative Southern Democrats became Republicans. The South had been mostly Democratic before 1964; it was mostly Republican after (Although on the local level continued to be heavily democratic for decades).
- Many "values voters" became Republicans. These were people who voted based on morality. They thought morally good things should be legal and morally bad things should be illegal. In the 1960s, sex was closely tied to morality. In this way, people who opposed abortion and gay rights, for example Jerry Falwell, and the changes to society happening in the 1960s and 70s, became Republicans.

- Republicans also made some gains among working-class Catholics, who are mostly conservative on social issues.
- The Democrats were able to make gains among more liberal Republicans and with Latino voters.
- Working-class Democrats voted for Republicans in the 1980 election. They were called Reagan Democrats because they voted for Ronald Reagan.

So, if you come across someone representing the current Republican Party as "The Party of Lincoln," remind them about the history of political party realignment.

SHOULD POLICE BE IMMUNIZED FROM LAWSUITS?

As a result of recent cases involving police use of excessive force, much has been said and written about the doctrine of qualified immunity, a defense that protects them from liability for damages unless their actions violate clearly established law. There are efforts currently under way to have this defense either revised or repealed, thereby holding those accountable for their actions presumably in the same manner as ordinary citizens.

There are other forms of immunity from liability, however. I am not aware of any effort to revise or repeal these immunities. The fundamental question is whether, by office or occupation, anyone should be immune from liability for their actions that harm others and, if so, to what extent.

Books have been written on the subject of immunity. Here, I've tried to distill, without either overgeneralizing or omitting, key points for your consideration. And I've tried to eliminate as much legalese as possible. What appears below is culled from several sources, and my own experiences in defending government action, frequently relying on these defenses. The purpose of this narrative is to allow you to do your own research and form your own conclusions about the legitimacy of these doctrines in today's society.

Sovereign Immunity

Sovereign immunity is a type of legal protection that prevents the United States and its departments, as well as state governments and their departments, from being sued for money damages in the case of tort claims (injury claims as a result of negligence) without their consent. Sovereign immunity is found in the Eleventh Amendment to the United States Constitution and, in Florida, Art. X, Sec. 13.

This judicial doctrine was adopted from the law of England before Parliament rose to power. The idea was that the crown was above the people, and English subjects could not file civil lawsuits against the monarchy or its agents. In early American history, the United States couldn't be sued either by states or by citizens without Congressional approval.

Today, although waivers and exceptions have been legalized by federal and state legislatures that authorize certain civil suits against the government, sovereign immunity remains intact. The reasoning behind sovereign immunity in the U.S. is that it is necessary to keep the government democratic, efficient, and effective; if this doctrine were not in place, the courts may be overwhelmed by civil claims, and the executive and legislative branches may not carry out their functions in fear of litigation.

In plain terms, sovereign immunity prevents the average citizen who may have been injured due to the government official's or employee's negligence from collecting monetary damages that they would otherwise be able to recover, if the civil suit was filed against another citizen or corporation.

Each state has its own sovereign immunity laws. Florida allows individuals to bring a tort claim against the state government when the state's employees' actions resulted in property loss, personal injuries, or wrongful deaths. However, there are three major limitations to this waiver (and multiple minor limitations).

The measure of damages that can be recovered in a case against the state is limited to $200,000 against one government agency or $300,000 against multiple government agencies. If a plaintiff believes that they are owed more than that amount, there is a complicated legal process by which they can file a petition with the Florida legislature and request more damages.

Employees of the state of Florida cannot be held personally liable unless their negligence was intentional (acted in bad faith, with malevolent intent, or infringed upon human rights).

Plaintiffs are prevented from collecting punitive damages or pre-judgement interest.

Even if a case involving sovereign immunity goes to trial, judges do not explain these three limitations to the jury. If a jury awards the plaintiff more than $200,000 or $300,00, no matter how much they award (say, $600,000), only $200,000 or $300,000 may be collected by the plaintiff.

Absolute Immunity

In United States law, absolute immunity is a type of sovereign immunity for government officials that confers complete immunity from criminal prosecution and suits for damages, so long as officials are acting within the scope of their duties. The Supreme Court of the United States has consistently held that government officials deserve some type of immunity from lawsuits for damages, and that the common law recognized this immunity. The Court reasons that this immunity is necessary to protect public officials from excessive interference with their responsibilities and from "potentially disabling threats of liability."

In the United States, absolute civil immunity applies to the following people and circumstances:

- lawmakers engaged in the legislative process;

- judges acting in their judicial capacity;
- government prosecutors while making charging decisions;
- executive officers while performing adjudicative functions;
- the President of the United States;
- Presidential aides who first show that the functions of their office are so sensitive as to require absolute immunity, and who then show that they were performing those functions when performing the act at issue;
- witnesses while testifying in court (although they are still subject to perjury);

Qualified Immunity

Qualified immunity is a type of legal immunity. "Qualified immunity balances two important interests—the need to hold public officials accountable when they exercise power irresponsibly and the need to shield officials from harassment, distraction, and liability when they perform their duties reasonably." It is a judicially crafted type of immunity.

Specifically, qualified immunity protects a government official from lawsuits alleging that the official violated a plaintiff's rights, only allowing suits where officials violated a "clearly established" statutory or constitutional right. When determining whether or not a right was "clearly established," courts consider whether a hypothetical reasonable official would have known that the defendant's conduct violated the plaintiff's rights. Courts conducting this analysis apply the law that was in force at the time of the alleged violation, not the law in effect when the court considers the case.

Qualified immunity is not immunity from having to pay money damages, but rather immunity from having to go through the costs of a trial at all. Accordingly, courts must resolve qualified immunity issues as early in a case as possible, preferably before discovery.

Qualified immunity only applies to suits against government officials as individuals, not suits against the government for damages caused by the officials' actions. Although qualified immunity frequently appears in cases involving police officers, it also applies to most other executive branch officials. While judges, prosecutors, legislators, and some other government officials do not receive qualified immunity, most are protected by other immunity doctrines as previously described.

NEWSPAPER EDITORIALS ARE ESSENTIAL IN A FREE SOCIETY

This is for those of you who read newspapers, with particular focus on the editorial page or pages, and specifically on editorials.

Newspapers' editorial opinions represent an important contribution to our understanding of the relationship between the press and politics. Editorials are a distinctive format and are the only place in a newspaper where the opinions of a paper as an organization are explicitly represented. The general consensus from my research and experience is that newspapers and the journalists who write editorials play a powerful role in generating political debate in the public sphere. They use their editorial voice to attempt to influence politics either indirectly, through formation of public opinion, or directly, by focusing on government officials. Editorials are at their most persuasive during elections, when newspapers traditionally declare support for candidates and political parties.

Editorials require a distinctive style and form of expression, occupy a special place in a newspaper, represent the collective institutional voice of a newspaper rather than that of an individual, usually have no bylines, and are written with differing aims and motivations to news articles. The historical development of journalism, from the obvious bias and rants from the earliest newspapers to the era of "yellow journalism" to the present, explains the status of editorials as a distinctive form of journalism. Over time, professional ideals and practices have evolved to demand objectivity in news reporting and the separation of fact from opinion. Many books and articles have been written on this very subject.

Researchers have attributed an important role to editorials in informing and shaping debate in four ways: (1) as an influence on readers, voters, and/or public opinion; (2) as an influence on the internal news agendas and coverage of newspapers; (3) as an influence on the agendas and coverage in other news media; and (4) as an influence on political or policy agendas. Although editorials have a long history in American journalism, there are challenges that lie ahead; challenges that relate to how professional norms respond to age-old questions about objectivity, bias, and partisanship in the digital age.

A newspaper editorial is typically found clearly set out in the medium, and reflects a collegial decision of the newspaper's editorial board. A newspaper editorial board is made up of experts in journalism who govern the tone and direction of the newspaper. Most newspapers have an editorial page. On that page the newspaper publishes its own opinions about current affairs, as well as the views of other writers and experienced and knowledgeable commentators, and letters written by the readers.

The Tallahassee Democrat, in addition to letters to the editor, citizen opinion articles and columns by expert commentators, also has a Zing! column where readers can submit anonymous attacks or criticisms briefly stated.

But the Democrat does not have is an editorial column, and does not endorse political candidates. While opinions are readily expressed by individual writers, there is nothing in the newspaper that reflects the opinion, wisdom or conscience of the <u>Democrat</u> as an institution discharging its role under the First Amendment as an historic defender of liberty and freedom and a bulwark against the corrupt or dishonest. If news articles and individual opinion columns alone discharged this overriding constitutional imprimatur, American journalism will not have a long and rich history of editorials. Note the Washington Post's succinct statement of the profound importance of a free press: "Democracy dies in darkness."

Three years ago, in February 2018, the <u>USA Today</u> noted that "the news department has an important task, which is to write a first draft of history as it happens; the opinion pages shape how we look at our history." While individual citizens and columnists wax on issues of public importance, they do not have the power--and do not command the attention of our elected and appointed leaders--that the voice of a community newspaper does through its editorials.

I recognize that it is a publisher's and editor's decision whether to publish editorials. However, from the vantage point of those in whose charge with put our faith and trust to provide for our health, safety and welfare, they are less inclined to be overly concerned about being held accountable by a letter to the editor or column—or even a Zing!--than by the strong, unified voice of the local newspaper. It is, after all, among the most vital responsibilities of the press to hold government accountable; to keep them honest as they discharge their duties, always remembering—or being reminded—that public office is a public trust. If the local press doesn't have this institutional community voice, then who does?

JOURNALISM MAY BE DEAD, JUST NOT IN A WAY READILY UNDERSTOOD

To those who believe journalism is dead, I agree, but not for the reasons they usually give. I believe that, too often, government hides information that casts it in a negative light. With the decline of newspapers, there is also a decline in the type of investigative reporting that led to Watergate, the Pentagon Papers, and other instances of government coverups.

I think there is an overarching reliance on press releases and laws that, in the name of protecting victims, are used to block the flow of information that is important to the public. A press release allows government to present information favorable to itself, leaving out the inconvenience of information that casts a negative light. When legitimate news is blocked from public consumption, the notion of an informed citizenry takes a hit.

Democracy depends on an informed citizenry, not one that is fed lies and beliefs masking as fact. The Washington Post has as its motto: "Democracy dies in darkness." This is so true, and the decline of a vigilant, aggressive press is an existential threat to Democracy.

I think most people would be surprised to learn that there are no education, training or experience requirements to become a journalist. Of course, it makes good sense to require a college degree in journalism, but this is a requirement that is imposed--if at all--by the hiring medium.

As with any proposal, the devil's in the details. How would a licensing system be set up? What would be the requirements to obtain a license? How long would the license last? Would there be some form of continuing education or training requirement? Obviously, the government can't be involved in any licensing plan; subjecting an independent press to political machinations would be a constitutional no-no. But even assuming some system of self-regulation among media were doable, how would it be set up? Would the top 20 newspapers (according to circulation) or the top 10 TV and radio markets (determined by the number of viewers) band together and come up with a set of standards that must be met before a license could be issued? Would the license be a national one, or issued state by state?

And even if this were to happen, what would prevent a newspaper, for example, from hiring a person who, although not licensed, was extremely knowledgeable in science and technology to write news articles on those subjects? Or any other subjects assigned by the editor? Could penalties be imposed and, if so, what kind and how would they be enforced? If a person is well educated, has an inquiring mind and can write decently, would he be barred from becoming a journalist because he fails to meet other standards?

You are both well aware of the famous statement that Democracy is the worst form of government except for all the others. This might well apply to any licensing system for journalists. It's frustrating when some of the so-called network news outlets pass off their commentators and pundits as news reporters, although they clearly aren't. And we all suffer the consequences of misinformation, disinformation and downright lying. But I suppose in the final analysis, it's going to be up to an educated, informed public to ultimately separate the wheat from the chaff. Of course, there have been times when this is more difficult than others.

We are in such a time right now but, to quote another time-worn phrase, "eternal vigilance is the price of liberty." We just have to hope that a system that has survived for almost 250 years will continue to do so. Sure, the ride has been bumpy, and there have been occasions when our very survival was at stake, but we're still here, chugging along and trying to be faithful to Ben Franklin's admonition that our Democracy can prevail, if we can keep it. Oh, and no, the government will never give journalists subpoena power. There are those who won't even acknowledge the power and authority of a congressional subpoena. As for lying, well, journalists have been calling out government lies since the nation's founding. Just keep it up; the liars can't stand the heat, and the result is a better-informed society.

THE SAD STATE OF AMERICAN PRINT JOURNALISM–AND A PERSONAL STORY

The loss of newspapers over the past several years should be a wakeup call for those who cherish our First Amendment's guarantee of a free press. Democracy depends on an informed citizenry; sadly, with the steady, relentless decline of newspapers, the flow of information designed to educate is reduced.

I have a particular interest in the state of American newspapers. My first professional love was journalism, and it came to me quite by accident.

I always wanted to be a lawyer. I watched Perry Mason on TV in the 1950s and 1960s and was enamored at how he won the case each week. (Of course, I didn't consider how he might have fared on the other four workdays.) Only one thing stopped me: finances.

I knew I would have to work for a while once I earned my bachelor's degree. With no great thought or plan, I applied to the University of Florida College of Education. I was taking political science classes and enjoyed them, so I thought I'd teach American history in high school to earn enough to eventually attend law school.

One of my required classes was American history. This was the only class I received less than a C; I missed that C by one point! Turns out the College of Education didn't accept

Ds for graduation, so I would have to re-take that class; however, since it wasn't offered again for another year, I would have to either remain in school (and pay additional tuition and incur a year of living expenses which neither my family nor I had) or go home, find a job and hope I would be re-admitted to the college to take this one class (and incur those additional expenses). In either event, I would have to postpone graduation by one year.

I didn't want to do that, so I searched for a program that would accept that D, and found the School of Journalism. I took the entire news reporter print journalism curriculum over one full year and graduated in August of 1965. I only lost two months from my originally planned graduation day.

Eventually, I took a job at the Palm Beach Post-Times and then the Fort Lauderdale News. As a reporter, I covered the police and court beats. I was fortunate to befriend several judges and other public officials who, upon learning of my interest in law, took me under their wing and wrote letters and made phone calls supporting my application. After about two years as a reporter, I made enough money to attend Florida State University's new law school starting in 1967.

I often remind myself how the entire trajectory of my life might have been different had I gotten that C. I would have remained in education, perhaps never attended law school, wouldn't have moved to Tallahassee, met my wife, had two children, etc. Try recalling something in your life that appeared so insignificant at that time, yet could have changed the course of your life.

Please excuse the aside. Back to the source of my distress.

A recent report on the state of local news from Northwestern's Medill School of Journalism, Media, Integrated Marketing Communications, tells the sad story. The United States continues to lose newspapers at a rate of two per week, further dividing the nation into wealthier, faster growing communities with access to local news, and struggling areas without.

According to this report, between the pre-pandemic months of late 2019 and the end of May 2022, more than 360 newspapers closed. Since 2005, the country has lost more than one-fourth of its newspapers and is on track to lose a third by 2025.

Most of the communities that have lost newspapers do not get a print or digital replacement, leaving 70 million residents — or a fifth of the country's population — either living in an area with no local news organizations, or one at risk, with only one local news outlet and very limited access to critical news and information that can inform their everyday decisions and sustain grassroots democracy. About seven percent of the nation's counties, or 211, now have no local newspaper. These areas are called "news deserts," and they are growing.

Surviving newspapers, especially dailies, have cut staff and circulation significantly under financial pressure, reducing their ability to fill the gap when communities lose their local papers. More and more dailies are also dropping seven-day-a-week delivery, as they pursue digital subscribers. Forty of the largest 100 daily newspapers now deliver a print edition six or fewer times a week; 11 deliver two times a week or less.

The cause of this precipitous decline can be summed up in one word: competition. But it's more complicated than that. Television's arrival in the 1950s began the decline of newspapers as most people's source of daily news. In the '50s, I lived in New York City, where its eight-plus million residents had as many as a dozen daily newspapers to choose from. But with mergers, that number dropped to seven. Now, there are four serving about that same number. Accompanying this decline was the decline in the variety of in-depth news information from which the public could choose.

Television was the first blow; the explosion of the Internet in the 1990s was the second, and increased the range of media choices available to the average reader while further cutting into newspapers' dominance as the source of news.

A great boon of this communications explosion was the variety of choices; the downside is that, as we have seen in recent years, the rise of misinformation. There are so many varying avenues of information that it's becoming more and more difficult for the audience to discern fact from fiction, truth from lies, etc. This has given fresh meaning to the old saw that a lie can travel around the world while the truth is putting on its shoes.

This trend shows no signs of abating. Suggestions to try to save what remains include stop living in the past and waiting for the glory of print to return; recognize that the old newspaper business model is dead; stop pretending it is the only industry with a big audience; get serious about classifieds again; and keep the best people.

As a news reporter, I was taught to get the facts and tell the story—the who, what, when, where, why and how. This must remain the polestar of the print journalist.

The major network newscasts each night devote about 21 minutes to actual reporting; advertising takes up the rest. Twenty-four-hour cable news services frequently repeat their newscasts, usually refreshing them as circumstances warrant.

But there is one thing TV news casts, 24-hour news services and radio news can't do—they don't have the time or resources to provide the audience with in-depth reporting.

The kind of detailed, fact-based reporting and accompanying analysis that serves the vital function of fully informing the citizenry can only be accomplished by a newspaper that publishes daily or weekly. (Of course, there are magazines that perform this function; however, the reader must wait a month for that information.)

I fear that if our nation loses the newspaper, we face giving life to the Washington Post's great lament: "Democracy dies in Darkness."

A NOTE ON APPROPRIATION OF FUNDS AND THEIR USE

When the government appropriates funds, those funds can only be used for the purposes set out in the appropriations bill and general law governing the subject of the appropriations. That's the general theory behind appropriations. If, for example, the appropriations act provides that funds appropriated for education shall only be used for education purposes, and the government receiving those funds decides to use the money for purposes unrelated to education, that would violate the law.

I think the federal government's claim is that the appropriated funds can't be withheld from the appropriated purpose of providing for education, which includes salaries for those responsible for discharging educational responsibilities. The state is countering, I believe, by saying once the funds are appropriated, the state may use the money however it sees fit, including denying salaries for those who support mask mandates.

If there is a conflict in these two positions, then the Supremacy Clause decides the matter in favor of the federal government. If there is no conflict, the state prevails. The overriding question from the federal government's standpoint, as I see it, is how the state's educational purposes are met by denying salaries to school board members for exercising their home rule police power in acting to protect the health, safety and welfare of its citizens.

The problem for the county school boards, however, is that the police power--the power to act, especially in times of emergencies, to provide this protection--is a product of the Tenth Amendment to the US Constitution which provides that powers not given exclusively to the federal government reside with the states, or to the people of the states. Does this provision empower the state to grant to local governments portions of the police power, or does the state constitution, through its home rule provision, grant police power to local governments independent of the state?

In a 1905 decision, the U.S. Supreme Court ruled that the "police power" of the states allows "reasonable regulations ... as will protect the public health and safety." Jacobson v. Massachusetts, 197 U.S. 11. What does this mean? In a state of emergency, the government can restrain and regulate certain rights and liberties—such as the freedom to travel— for the greater good. But actions taken must be reasonable and use the least restrictive means (or methods). So, while generally, the government cannot restrict your movements, in the interest of health and safety, the government could temporarily limit or suspend your right to travel through shelter-in-place orders. Court battles are usually waged over what constitutes "reasonableness" in the exercise of police powers. I hope this lengthy narrative helps to answer your questions.

HAVE CONSERVATIVES BEEN ON THE RIGHT SIDE OF HISTORY? WHEN?

This is the question that I have been asking every time conservatives pat themselves on the back saying they're in the right: When have the conservatives been on the right side of history? Supporting slavery in the name of states' rights? NO. Supporting laissez-faire free economics at the turn of the 20th century? NO. (Remember the Great Depression?) Supporting Social Security and other New Deal programs designed to bolster a depressed economy to get us out of the Depression? NO. (The Republican Party is about big business, not the individual.)

How about their support for isolationism and America First during WW II? NO. (When Pearl Harbor was attacked, we weren't ready for war. Thankfully, the Democratic administration of FDR got us ready in time.) Supporting Medicare, Medicaid and Voting Rights legislation in the 1960s? NO. (The Republicans have historically opposed government involvement in public health, and we all know their stand on voting rights.)

How about government ethics? NO. (Remember Watergate and Iran-Contra?) Trickledown economics? NO. (Businesses are not designed to spread the wealth to the workers. They are in business to make money, and the more the merrier.) How about their relationship with labor and the right for groups to organize for health, safety and welfare purposes? NO. (The Republicans are for big business, but will fight every effort to allow for even close to a level playing field for laborers.)

This is a good summary of the Republican Party over the years. And today? Well, they oppose voting rights, academic freedom, teaching history with all of its warts and failings, home rule for local governments (but scream bloody murder when the federal government tries the same approach to the states; and on and on. Again, they continue to be on the wrong side of history.

They claim they're the party of Lincoln and believe in freedom, liberty and individual responsibility. Except that the current version of the party is anathema to Lincoln. Except that in the name of freedom and liberty, they continue to deny it to the greater mass of the population. In the name of individual responsibility, they are trying mightily to have you forget what happened last January 6 when the Capitol was attacked, even stonewalling or ignoring legitimate investigations.

Did I mention their claim to be the party of law and order? Well, remind them of that attack by their supporters on dozens of law enforcement officers during that fateful January 6 insurrection....which they even refuse to acknowledge was an assault. They can continue to deny, deflect and delay, and they can certainly convince some of the people some of the time, but they can't fool all of the people all of the time. The truth has a stubborn way of eventually coming out. And it will come out.

CONSERVATIVES AND LIBERALS: A COMPARISON

In the 1920s, conservative economic policies led to the stock market crash of 1929, and the Great Depression.

Liberals enacted programs in the 1930s, such as Social Security, designed to get our economy back on track.

In the 1930s, conservatives favored appeasing Adolf Hitler, refusing critical aid to Great Britain.

Liberals aided Great Britain in its "darkest hour" and with the allies, defeated Hitler, Nazism and Fascism in World War II.

Since 2017, conservatives have endorsed white nationalist, neo-Nazi groups.

Liberals oppose these groups, saying there is no place in America for Nazism, Fascism or any other form of repressive, authoritarian government.

In 2021, conservatives led an attack on the nation's capital, seeking to overthrow the government and keep Donald Trump in power unconstitutionally and illegally, based on a lie now known as the Big Lie.

Liberals (and some moderate conservatives) are trying to hold these self-professed conservative "law and order" champions accountable and responsible for their criminal conduct.

Conservatives are dishonoring subpoenas, pleading the Fifth Amendment, and obstructing justice, claiming what happened on January 6 was nothing more than "legitimate public discourse."

Liberals (and some moderate conservatives) are trying to get these conservatives to adhere to the rule of law and be true to their claim of favoring individual accountability and responsibility.

Conservatives have re-written election laws designed to suppress targeted voting groups, and are seeking the Supreme Court's blessing on a theory that would allow state legislatures to override the will of the voting public in federal elections.

Liberals (and some moderate conservatives) believe the right to vote is a fundamental constitutional right set out in several amendments, and that conservatives are undermining this fundamental right, which would be irrevocably undermined if conservative state legislatures are given the power to reject the will of the state voters... which is precisely what Donald Trump, and his loyalists, wanted some states to do in 2020.

Conservatives are re-writing history. declaring in law what can and can't be taught; declaring in law what can and can't be said in the classroom and on college and university campuses.

Liberals are resisting conservative efforts at undermining our nation's historic commitment to teaching history's important lessons, warts and all; they vigorously support academic freedom and are resisting conservative efforts to undermine classroom instruction.

Conservatives favor banning books.

Liberals oppose any and all efforts at thought control by book banning.

Conservatives favor the church directing the state, or a theocracy.

Liberals favor a wall of separation between church and state that has sustained our nation since its founding.

Conservatives seek to undermine constitutional privacy rights.

Liberals believe in the protection of individual privacy rights as fundamental in an ordered society.

Conservatives favor making access to firearms more convenient, including concealed and open carry in places where the public congregates--even as the number of mass shootings is rising, and with more and more being killed and injured by gunfire. Liberals favor common sense gun regulations, such as banning weapons of war on the streets, and restrictive registration requirements to avoid loopholes.

PLANT A TREE, HAVE A CHILD, WRITE A BOOK—THAT'S IMMORTALITY

Many years ago, as a young man, the father of a friend of mine told me something that has stuck with me over the years, and still resonates today. He said every man should do three things in his life: plant a tree, have a child, and write a book.

As I mulled this over in my mind, I thought how relatively simple it seemed to accomplish all three, but then I move on and didn't give it much more thought until I reached adulthood.

One day, after I married and was awaiting the birth of my first child, I recalled what I was told years earlier, so I decided to find the source of his words of wisdom. It turns out that's exactly what they were: words of wisdom.

The quote is: "Every man (or more correctly, person) should plant a tree, have a child, and write a book." It is attributed to the Talmud (the primary source of Jewish religious law and Jewish theology) and Jose Martí, Cuban revolutionary and poet. Other authors have waxed on it, most notably Ernest Hemingway.

Why these three things? These all live on after us, ensuring a measure of immortality.

Life is short. Each of us gets one shot at it. There are no do-overs, no replays (instant or otherwise) and no second chances to start over. There is no guarantee at birth that each of us will live from childhood to adulthood to old age. It is well to do the best we can, the most we can, while we can.

Planting a tree means giving back to the Earth whatever each person has taken from it. A tree will also survive generations and seed itself, allowing for growth of generations of more trees. If the tree is taken for wood, that product will be used to build a house or some other item that will last longer than the life of the person who planted that tree. In this way, immortality of the planter is assured.

You may be familiar with "plant a tree" programs. The Nature Conservancy's Plant a Billion Trees campaign is a major forest restoration program. Our goal is to plant a billion trees across the planet to slow the connected crises of climate change and biodiversity loss.

If you haven't planted your tree yet, or want to plant more, this is one of many programs that serve this purpose. There are others that can be found simply by checking the various websites.

Having and raising a child provides the knowledge that even after we are gone our legacy lives on through our offspring. Depression and war prevented my father from living his dream. He wanted his children--my late brother and me--to live the kind of life denied to him. Although his struggles and frustrations were many, his expectations for us were high. It didn't matter what we wanted to be; he just wanted us to excel at it. He instilled in us a strong value system, compelling us to behave in a certain manner: study hard, work hard, have gratitude and compassion, marry sensibly, have a home and children. In essence, what he wanted was for his children to fulfill his own unfinished dreams through them.

I have a feeling that this story isn't an isolated one.

The third path to immortality is writing a book. This shows unique intelligence, knowledge and literacy necessary to prepare a lengthy written composition. It is your own work, perhaps influenced by others, but set out in your own personal style.

I would include other written forms that have the same permanent effect as a book. For example, songs, poetry, plays and articles. Many of our greatest songwriters, poets and playwrights never wrote a book, yet their works stand the test of time. Articles reflecting the author's expertise or interest also serve as a permanent written exemplar of one's intelligence, knowledge, experience, etc. I wrote hundreds of byline articles as a newspaper reporter and editor, and dozens of law-related articles in my career, but never wrote a book.

That is, until 2012 when I wrote my first one while recovering from major orthopedic surgery. It was a memoir for my family, especially my children and grandchildren. This was followed by two novellas and a second memoir. Two years ago, I started writing extensively on social media. I retained each Facebook post and have written three books that consist of those posts, and I'm currently working on the fourth that will, of course, include this post.

A reputable publishing company ensures that each book is: provided its copyright date, deposited in the Library of Congress with an assigned number, and made available to such book sellers as Barnes and Noble and Amazon, as well as the publishing company itself.

There you have it. No need to search for the magic elixir of life, or visit St. Augustine and drink from the Fountain of Youth (I have. Several times. It doesn't work.). The path to immortality is in three parts. If you haven't yet planted a tree, do so. It's easy, especially if you have a backyard.

If you haven't written that book, published a song. poem, play or article, get going on it. Each of us has led a unique life. What not tell your story? Once you draft an outline in chronological form, you will be surprised how easy the words will flow. Trust me on this, I know because I did precisely that.

I'll leave the childbearing part to you.

THE VALUE OF PETS IN OUR LIVES

Each day I check my wife's and my Facebook page, we invariably find at least a couple of posts devoted to pets. The post might be about shirts worn by pet owners, or some comment about what a cat or dog did that was cute, funny or outlandish.

There are generally two types of pets: caged and roaming. Hamsters, gerbils, guinea pigs, mice, birds are caged; dogs and cats are the most prominent that roam through the house doing things dogs and cats do.

There have been books about how important pets are to our well-being, and it has been shown that you can judge the character of a person by how he/she treats an animal, particularly a dog or cat.

As a child, I didn't have any pets. They weren't allowed in the New York City brownstones and federal housing projects where I lived. It wasn't until I was on my own working as a news reporter in Fort Lauderdale that I had my first pet, a hamster.

After I married, settled down and had two children, it took my youngest daughter Amy to convince me to have a pet beyond the caged guinea pig, rabbit and mouse.

Amy worked as a vet tech and told us about a cat that needed a home. With some careful persistence on Amy's part, Rudy joined our family. Shortly thereafter, again with Amy's persistence, we took Jolly in as a rescue cat. Amy was also taking horse riding lessons from a woman who bred Shar-Peis. Mama shar-pei was about to deliver, and Amy was given the pick of the litter. I resisted, as I did rather timidly with the two cats, recalling my upbringing in New York where dogs growled and menaced the neighborhood, or so I believed. But Amy persisted again and I finally relented; Amy picked this adorable ball of dark fur that we named Pepper. The sale was sealed when I held this ball of fur and had this little tongue lick my face.

Rudy and Jolly were older male cats; very cuddly and affectionate. Pepper was born with conditions that are somewhat unique to the breed. The sad news for us was they don't live very long lives, usually about eight years or so.

Rudy and Jolly lived full lives, each passing at about 19. Pepper, thanks to the loving care and attention she received, survived to age 11.

After we lost our three pets, we vowed not to have anymore—until we visited our vet just a few days after we lost Pepper.

We saw two little balls of fur curled up together in the vet's front window. I asked my wife Harriet which one she wanted. She said we can't separate them, which I knew she would say. We took home a tan and black girl we named Sandy, and a dark, long-haired girl we named Mandy.

Our vet told us that there's a vast difference between boy and girl cats. We found that out rather quickly. Those of you familiar with this story know that girl cats are more particular and finicky than their male counterparts. If a female wants your attention, it's on her time, not yours.

So, we were back to two cats again. That was 11 years ago. They are still with us as independent as ever. They eat when they're hungry, even if they have to wake up Harriet to feed them. I get the job of moving them off my pillow when I want to lie down.

Two years ago, I wrote about how Moo and his sister, Floof, came into our lives and joined our family in November of 2020, when they were barely two months old. We never had kittens at such a young age, and we enjoyed how the two of them played together, scampering through the house, jumping from chair to table to counter (driving our two older cats to distraction), curious about their surroundings, getting into everything, and generally doing all things little kittens do.

We were now a family of four felines, three girls and one boy.

Shortly after we brought them home, we took them to our vet for examination and kitty shots. And then we received devastating news that Moo tested positive for feline leukemia. Prognosis is 3-5 years.

We vowed that we would give Moo the best life we could, making sure he got the best medical care available.

A few weeks later, Moo had an attack. He was gasping for air and threw up. But it passed that day, he resumed kitten antics, and we thought nothing further about it. However, the next day, he had another attack, only this time he ejected mucous. We immediately made an appointment with our vet and took Moo in for examination, including an x-ray.

When we saw the x-ray, we were shocked. A huge baseball-size lymphoma had formed in Moo's chest cavity and was pressing on his esophagus; he was at risk for suffocation. The doctor said surgery was out; he wouldn't survive that. Chemo and steroids wouldn't reduce the size of the tumor. The vet didn't have to tell us about options; we could see in her eyes what had to be done.

Harriet and I were devastated. A few hours ago, Moo was an active little kitten. Now, we had but a few precious moments to say goodbye.

Moo had given us so much joy and laughter. He was the ringleader of our four felines. He made our two senior cats stare in wonder as he frolicked through our home; and his frequent tussles with his sister delighted us, giving one another a lifetime playmate. Or so we thought.

Through our sobs and tears, Harriet held Moo in her arms, and I petted him as the vet injected him. Moo let out a yelp and then fell still. After a second injection, which Moo didn't feel, she checked his breathing and said he was gone.

As we have done for our previous three pets that we lost, we had him cremated, ordered a stone and buried him next to them. Moo's stone carries this message that is all so true: "pawprints on our hearts."

Losing Moo was different. While Pepper, Rudy and Jolly lived full lives, Moo was with us only 2 ½ months. Our first three pets were ill and at the end of their lives; we had time to say our goodbyes. Moo was active and full of life even on his last day, when we were faced with the grim reality that his genetic line deprived our little one of his life. We now know all too well the pain of losing such a small, loving pet at such a young age.

But as pets do, Moo taught us something about ourselves. In fact, each of our pets taught us this great lesson. They are God's little creatures who give us unrequited love in return for what is hoped will be loving and caring owners. Studies have shown that pet ownership is good for one's mental and emotional health. They help reduce stress and keep you engaged. They are wonderful companions.

We know Moo never had chance; that x-ray told us his life was over. But it doesn't lessen the pain of losing a pet we loved, especially one so young and full of life.

As for Floof, since our older cats live in their own orbit, Moo's sister gets plenty of love and attention whenever she allows us to give it. She is the most curious cat I've ever seen, and isn't afraid when someone knocks on our door or comes in to visit us. Mandy and Sandy scamper off and hide under the bed in our bedroom.

Yes, it hurts to lose a pet, and since they don't live as long as we do, losing a pet is part of life. But while they're with us, they teach us about love and devotion, and how fragile life is. There really is no greater lesson.

PRESIDENTIAL LEADERSHIP

As debate rages over the conduct of recent presidents, it is appropriate to consider their performance against the generally recognized leadership qualities that inform how presidents do their job. Historians who have ranked presidents over the years have generally found several principles of performance, allowing them to rate them from great to average to mediocre.

World renown historian and author Doris Kerns Goodwin visited Florida State University last night to discuss "Presidential Leadership in Turbulent Times." This subject is also the title of her book published in 2018 that discusses the leadership styles and skills of Abraham Lincoln, Theodore Roosevelt, Franklin Roosevelt and Lyndon Johnson.

Many books have been written detailing the turbulent times each of these four president endured, and the skills they possessed to deal with them. Although certainly not without fault, these men exhibited the character and commitment necessary to accept the challenges of their time and move the nation forward.

Her address to a sold-out university audience was about the past, but it was also about our future. History talks to the present, telling us how we might avoid the pitfalls of the past so that we can prepare for a bright and prosperous future. But if we fail to heed the harsh lessons of the past, we are condemned to repeat them.

The focus of her lecture was presidential leadership. With this in mind, it's worthwhile to consider what presidential leadership is, and compare those characteristics with those who have held the highest office in the land, as well as those who aspire to someday reside temporarily in the White House.

Whether we want to be or not, we are all impacted by that elected official who is the most powerful person in the world. His policies that become law affect all of us one way or another. So, it's important that we choose for that office someone who meets the qualities listed below.

James David Barber, in his book, "The Presidential Character: Predicting Performance in the White House," echoes other noted historians in setting out some common leadership qualities that successful presidents appear to have in common.

They are:

- A strong vision for the country's future
- An ability to put their own times in the perspective of history
- Effective communication skills
- The courage to make unpopular decisions
- Crisis management skills
- Character and integrity
- Wise appointments
- An ability to work with Congress

The criteria have varied over the years, and historians hesitate to include recent presidents because they want these men to have more of a track record to go by. But those presidents who consistently rate at the top are Abraham Lincoln, George Washington, and Franklin Roosevelt. Others who consistently rank high include Thomas Jefferson, Andrew Jackson, Theodore Roosevelt, Woodrow Wilson, and Harry Truman. Match the criteria above with each president and the relationship is self-evident. The most recent ranking of presidents include each of these men among the top 12. Also on that list are Dwight Eisenhower, Ronald Reagan and Barack Obama.

Historians who last ranked the presidents in 2001 used these criteria:

Public Persuasion
Crisis Leadership
Economic Management
Moral Authority
International Relations
Administrative Skills
Relations with Congress
Vision / Setting an Agenda
Pursued Equal Justice For All
Performance Within Context of Times

Barber defines those characteristics great presidents and leaders have in common. There is an evident overlap between his list and the ones noted above. Some identify the same characteristic, but use different words. As you read this, compare those presidents over the past 30 years and ask how many match the criteria for effective leadership by our nation's chief executive, how many have strengths and weaknesses, and how many fail the leadership test:

1. They provide clarity.

Being clear about what needs to be done – and concisely expressing business visions and goals – is vital for effective leadership. Employees need to know where the organization is headed and what the expectations are for getting there, both from an individual and team perspective.

2. They listen and allow others to be heard.

Good leaders listen closely with the goals of understanding others and being understood. Effective listeners gain access to a diversity of ideas and potential solutions that otherwise would not have been generated. They also strengthen relationships, build trust, improve teamwork and show employees that they care.

3. They value conversations.

Effective communication is important, but it requires more than just a basic oral or written transaction between two people. Good leaders facilitate genuine conversations – meaningful human-to-human connections – and bring people together to work and gain agreement in order to achieve goals.

4. They model desired behaviors.

Quite simply, strong leaders walk the walk and talk the talk. In other words, they model the same behavior they expect from their teams. You can have inspirational quotes and company values framed on the wall all you want, but modeled behavior will always be more effective.

5. They encourage healthy conflict.

Healthy conflict is good for relationships and organizations because it challenges assumptions and creates great results. Powerful leaders allow different views to be presented and shared, and know that disagreements can open pathways to innovation and higher-performing teams.

6. They create an environment of emotional safety.

Successful organizations consist of employees who are invested in their work, which means there will be moments of joy, frustration, confusion, exhaustion, and a host of other feelings. Emotions, both positive and negative, are a fundamental part of who we are, and ignoring or suppressing them is harmful. Good leaders know the importance of fostering a healthy cognitive and emotional culture, in which individuals feel safe in saying how they feel and expressing their views, without stigma or shame.

7. They have high levels of self-awareness.

It's important for leaders to be aware of their own strengths, weaknesses, tendencies, preferences and other personality traits, because these characteristics have a significant impact on how they behave and interact with others. Leaders with high levels of self-awareness can consciously influence situations and positively affect their teams. Leaders that are not self-aware make decisions and behave in ways that can lead to undesirable or negative consequences.

8. They empower others.

Successful business leaders are confident in their own hiring decisions, and give employees the freedom they need to come up with innovative ideas, initiatives or processes on their own. Those who micromanage only serve to limit creativity and potential, which demoralizes employees and contributes to a frustrated and low-functioning workforce.

9. They welcome feedback.

Giving and receiving feedback can feel uncomfortable, but failing to do so could seriously hurt the company or organization. Unchecked inefficiencies and practices will hamper growth. Learning to embrace honest feedback with an open mind and the willingness to improve where necessary will make individuals, teams and the business stronger. Additionally, when leaders routinely expose themselves to candid feedback, it makes it easier for employees to do the same.

Compare these nine qualities with the following list of qualities for a great leader in any endeavor: vision, inspiration, strategic and critical thinking, interpersonal communication, authenticity and self-awareness, open-mindedness and creativity, flexibility, responsibility and dependability, patience and tenacity, and continuous improvement.

As you praise or condemn past presidents, use the criteria above to support your position.

INDOCTRINATON AND BRAINWASHING. WHAT'S THE DIFFERENCE?

Both words are being tossed around as weapons to justify one's beliefs while castigating others. They have become a form of epithets that are supposed to explain what the "other side" is suffering from. However, what is missing is a basic understanding of what these words actually mean. It is admittedly impossible to discuss the depth of meaning of these words. Books have been written about both words, their meanings, applications, etc.

In this light, here are some basic definitions and examples of both words. The next time you hear or see them, you will have some idea what the speaker or writer is talking about—assuming they know.

Indoctrination means "to imbue with a usually partisan or sectarian opinion, point of view, or principle; to instruct especially in fundamentals or rudiments."

Examples of indoctrination "include hiding facts, disparaging student opinions, or rejecting any ideas that contradict the teacher's beliefs. Indoctrination is a means of forcing, brainwashing, or imposing desired ideologies without open discussion."

Indoctrination techniques include the use of propaganda, brainwashing, censorship and other restrictions on freedom of expression and information, advertising, angled phrasing and contents of government and official information, with monopoly of the media."

Brainwashing is "a forcible indoctrination to induce someone to give up basic political, social, or religious beliefs and attitudes and to accept contrasting regimented ideas; persuasion by propaganda or salesmanship.

Brainwashing is commonly associated with cults and abuse. A cult leader might, for example, present a warm and friendly disposition to gain a person's trust, then slowly break down the person by calling him or her names, forcing him or her to work, and engaging in other forms of abuse.

Common features of brainwashing include isolation, humiliation, accusation, and unpredictable attacks.

Someone who is brainwashed rarely questions things that they're told by their leader or the person they look up to, and they often don't have their own opinions. Helping someone who's brainwashed can be challenging, and it can take a long time since their ideas are deeply rooted in their mind.

In psychology, the study of brainwashing, often referred to as thought reform, falls into the sphere of "social influence." Social influence happens every minute of every day. It's the collection of ways in which people can change other people's attitudes, beliefs and behaviors. For instance, the compliance method aims to produce a change in a person's behavior and is not concerned with his attitudes or beliefs. It's the "Just do it" approach. Persuasion, on the other hand, aims for a change in attitude, or "Do it because it'll make you feel good/happy/healthy/successful." The education method (which is called the "propaganda method" when you don't believe in what's being taught) goes for the social-influence gold, trying to affect a change in the person's beliefs, along the lines of "Do it because you know it's the right thing to do." Brainwashing is a severe form of social influence that combines all of these approaches to cause changes in someone's way of thinking without that person's consent and often against his will."

Four signs of a brainwashed person are: They're no longer themselves; they've turned into someone else. They are obsessed with their new beliefs, group, and the group leader; they can't stop talking about these. They have a strong attachment to their new beliefs. They follow the group leader unthinkingly, sometimes to their own detriment.

Indoctrination and brainwashing are near synonyms; however, indoctrination is a much older (17th century) word which originally merely meant "teach," applied mainly to the teaching of religion; brainwashing as a word did not appear until the 1950s." At that time, brainwashing was used to describe how the Chinese government appeared to make people cooperate with them. Research into the concept also looked at Nazi Germany, at some criminal cases in the United States, and at the actions of human traffickers. In the late 1960s and 1970s, there was considerable scientific and legal debate about its use in the conversion of people to groups that are considered to be cults.

There is a difference between education and brainwashing. "Education informs learners about the facts around them and helps them become critical thinkers. In contrast, brainwashing provides learners with heavily biased information that leads to one predetermined conclusion."

BETTE DAVIS WAS RIGHT: "GETTING OLD ISN'T FOR SISSIES."

This take on a line from screen legend Bette Davis just about sums up where I am today. Yesterday, I visited one of my orthopedic doctors (yes, I've had several over the years) for injections to ease my low back pain. To echo the words from Alcoholics Anonymous, "I am an Arthritic."

Now, lots of folks have arthritis, especially those of us who have reached senior citizen status. But some have more arthritis than others. That's me. Lucky me.

I figure my parents had a choice: they could have left me with their millions, or their osteoarthritic conditions. Well, they really didn't have a choice; since they didn't have millions. So, they left me with the only other thing they both had--a lifetime of these memories that I would gladly sell if I had two things, the ability to sell and a willing masochistic buyer. Well, it is an inheritance, isn't it?

As a child, I remember asking my dad why he was so stooped over. He told me what his mom told him when he asked her: "Well, that's where the money is." Dad said you'll have a far better chance finding that dollar bill on the ground than standing straight up. Of course, stooped shoulders is a product of age; when arthritis is added to the mix, well, you get the picture. When the pain increases, I find myself stooped over, spending more and more time looking at the ground. I've actually picked up a few pennies, nickels, dimes and quarters over the years, and there was that $20 bill I found in a parking lot, so my grandma certainly spoke words of great wisdom.

My first introduction to arthritis was when I was 38. I was shaving one morning and, as I tried to stand up from leaning over the sink, got this sharp, stabbing pain in my lower back. An emergency visit to my first orthopedist and a few days of ice and naproxen eased the pain. (These days, when I take Aleve, I remind myself that I took both naproxen and ibuprofen when they were prescription medications. In fact, over the years, I've had prescribed just about every pain pill and NSAIDs on the market.)

Since then, I've had five knee surgeries, both knees replaced, right shoulder replaced, eight other shoulder surgeries, several surgeries for trigger fingers, both thumbs rebuilt— more than two dozen orthopedic surgeries by eight different doctors.

I also had seven vertebrae in my neck and upper back fused so that I no longer have lateral head movement. This resulted from a condition called Forestier's disease. Picture your spine as a candelabra. Now, picture hot, dripping wax pouring over that candelabra. That was the condition of my spine 12 years ago. My spine was deteriorating, and would have fused automatically over a few years—an extremely painful few years. So, it was a choice of immediate fusion or years of intense pain. Great choice, eh? To this day, I live with neck pain for which I see a neurologist who injects Botox into my neck four times each year to ease the pain.

I am jokingly called the Bionic Man by the wonderful folks at the Tallahassee Orthopedic Center. Personally, I think I deserve a wing bearing my name.

I think that when we reach a certain age, all of us have to visit an "ist" of one kind or another. Oncologist, rheumatologist, cardiologist, you get the point. Well, for me, I suppose I'm very lucky: I have only two "ists" that I see regularly, the orthopedist who is a pain management physician who handles, well, pain management, and the neurologist for Botox injections. Lots of needles. (There's also a urologist that I see for annual checkups, and my primary physician who makes sure all systems are functioning properly—or at least as properly as they can as I near 80, but that's it.)

The key here is that it's all about pain management. I'll never be free of pain; that's the toll arthritis takes. However, the degree of pain can be managed. I get inflammatory flareups. When they hit, the pain increases. As I get older, these flareups become more frequent, more intense and last longer.

The key to dealing with arthritis pain is to keep moving. Even when the pain is great, movement is essential, otherwise there is great risk in a downward cycle of the joint freezing into its continually deteriorating position. But when exercise, physical therapy and medication no longer ease the pain, and surgery can't be performed when there is significant arthritis (as in my lower back), injections are what's left in the physician's tool bag. And movement even when you don't want to do anything. For me, it's a three-mile walk at a moderate pace every other day at the Premier track, and one hour of aerobic exercises in the pool in between. These exercises actually do reduce the pain level, albeit temporarily.

I get upset when I read directions on OTC medications: "For temporary relief." Who the hell wants only temporary relief? I look for the day when medicine announces a pain pill that is advertised as "For permanent relief." Yeah, right.

I guess I should consider myself lucky that I'm not a patient for those doctors who treat the serious stuff, but there are days......

Next up for me is what the orthopedists call radiofrequency ablation, or rhizotomy. In laymen's terms, this involves use of a needle to kill nerve ends, those pesky pain transmitters that cause so much trouble. I had this procedure over 10 years ago and it worked. There's every reason it will work again, hopefully for 10 more years. Then I can look forward to this helpful procedure every 10 years. Now that's optimism.

After I had my neck fused and faced a couple of years of recovery, I took Neil Sedaka's great song "Breaking Up is Hard to Do," and wrote a parody. I'll end this note for those who are musically inclined (and those who aren't) with my feelings back then:

(Chorus: Down doo-be-doo fall down, a downa downa down doo-be-doo fall down, a downa downa down doo-be-doo fall down, getting old is hard to do.)

Please take these pains away from me
Arthritis leaves me in misery
All these aches just make me blue
Getting old is hard to do.
Years ago, I had no pain,
Now I think it's just so insane
After all that I go through
Yes, getting old is hard to do,
I said that getting old is hard to do
Hard to hear, and hard to chew
Don't say that this is my fate
Don't tell me getting old is really all that great
I won't give in, I'm a stubborn guy
No need to give a reason why
Joint replacement and orthopedic shoes
Yes, getting old is hard to do.

OK, it's not Johnny Mercer, Cole Porter, Carole King, or even Bud Abbott and Lou Costello. (Actually, considering what passes for good lyrics these days, perhaps my effort isn't so bad.)

But all things considered--my family, my friends, my career, things I've done, I'll take the arthritis if I must. I'll just manage it to the best of my ability, do the best I can each day, and keep my eyes on the future.

In the immortal words of Yankee great Lou Gehrig,

"I consider myself the luckiest man on the face of the earth."

___

JUDICIAL INTERPRETATION OF THE CONSTITUTION

Having argued many cases on constitutional law during my more than 40 years of active practice in both federal and state court, including the United States Supreme Court and Florida Supreme Court, I believe I have a certain understanding of how this is accomplished.

At the outset, note that nowhere in the United States Constitution is there any description of how it is to be interpreted. The Court, in Marbury v. Madison (1803) established the principle of judicial review in the United States, meaning that American courts have the power to strike down laws and statutes that violate the Constitution.

In the 219 years that have passed since then, the Court hasn't set out how constitutional issues should be decided.

What has developed over the years are two overriding schools of thought on constitutional interpretation. It is admittedly difficult to capture every element of these two interpretive approaches. In the interest of avoiding hyper-technicalities, I offer these thumbnail descriptions to highlight their meanings.

One school is called the originalists, or textualists. This is the method used by conservatives who believe that the words of the Constitution can only mean what the framers intended them to mean when it was adopted. Justice Antonin Scalia was one of the most forceful modern advocates for originalism, a theory that treats the Constitution like a statute, and gives it the meaning that its words were understood to mean at the time of adoption. As a textualist, Justice Scalia totally rejected reliance on legislative history or legislative intent. As he said in 2008: "It's what did the words mean to the people who ratified the Bill of Rights or who ratified the Constitution." In explaining his theory of interpretation, he said the Constitution is a "dead" document.

This designation is in direct opposition to the second school of thought on constitutional interpretation, living constitutionalism or judicial pragmatism. This concept or theory is relied on by liberals and is based on the notion that the Constitution has relevant meaning beyond the original text and is an evolving and dynamic document that changes over time as societal conditions change over time. In sum, the Constitution as a "living" document requires that the views of contemporaneous society should be considered when interpreting key constitutional phrases.

Predictably, those who favor one theory oppose the other.

Retiring Justice Stephen Breyer has recently criticized the "originalist" approach, calling on judges to focus more on the Constitution's goal of an active, participatory democracy, noting that this approach can be at odds with that goal. Anti-originalists point out that by interpreting the Constitution at the time of its adoption, and its amendments at their time of adoption, some basic rights such as abortion, same-sex marriage, interracial marriage, contraception, privacy, and others associated with the living constitutionalist theory would not exist today. They also contend that interpreting the Constitution in accordance with long outdated views is often unacceptable as a policy matter, and therefore an evolving interpretation is necessary. Another view is that the constitutional framers specifically wrote the Constitution in broad and flexible terms to create such a dynamic, "living" document.

Supporters of originalism argue that the Constitution should be changed through the amendment process, and that the living constitutionalism theory can be used by judges to inject their personal values into constitutional interpretation, thus the label of an "activist" judge who "legislates from the bench."

But consistency has been called the last refuge of the unimaginative, and proponents of both theories have on occasion crossed over to the other side to reach a particular result. At bottom, an activist judge is one who issues an opinion others disagree with. It's a convenient label that is easy to attach and easy to be accepted without thought. Believing that judicial activism is only found in one theory is a myth.

ART DOES IMITATE LIFE

Remember the television show All in the Family? It was a comedy but also a social commentary that ran from 1971 to 1979 and featured four main characters. The lead character, Archie Bunker, was portrayed as a loudmouthed, uneducated bigot who typified every conceivable stereotype. His wife, Edith, was sweet but, well, a few bricks shy of a load. Remember Archie calling her a dingbat?

They and their daughter, Gloria, and her husband, Mike Stivic, all lived in a working-class home. Archie couldn't avoid the people he disdained. His son-in-law, whom Archie called "Meathead," was an unemployed student of Polish descent who fit the classic stereotype of a liberal; the Jeffersons next door were black; Edith's cousin Maude was a feminist (the Jeffersons and Maude had their own spinoff series). Later in the show, Archie's partners in a local tavern were Jewish.

It was a top-rated show that focused on Archie's rants about all things liberal. The overriding purpose of the show was to see the humor in Archie's rants. (Do you know any Archies?)

Do you remember the opening theme? It went like this:

> Boy the way Glen Miller played,
> Songs that made the hit parade,
> Guys like us we had it made,
> Those were the days,
> And you know where you were then,
> Girls were girls and men were men,
> Mister we could use a man like Herbert Hoover again,
> Didn't need no welfare states
> Everybody pulled his weight,
> Gee our old Lasalle ran great,
> Those were the days.

The show aired during the latter part of the Vietnam War, after both the civil rights and voting rights acts were passed during President Lyndon Johnson's "Great Society" years. This song was a harkening back to the days of post-World War I to the end of the Roaring 20s.

You recall how the 20s ended: the Great Depression, followed by the greatest wave of social welfare legislation in our nation's history. That wave has never been duplicated because we never faced another economic crisis so deep.

Art does indeed imitate life. Another television example of this is the great Twilight Zone anthologies of the 1960s, written primarily by Rod Serling. who well understood the human condition and human nature. Both All in the Family and the Twilight Zone made us look at ourselves-- our anger, our fears, our prejudices.

Today, there are forces that want us to return to the days referenced in the All in the Family theme and demonstrated by the show's main character. These forces champion themselves in the Archie Bunker mode (although they would never admit it) with Mike as the convenient out-of-touch liberal foil.

If history is indeed cyclical and these forces prevail, we can expect a return to those "glory days" of post-World War I to the 20s, and those of the post-World War II era as well.

Remember the House Un American Activities Committee and its efforts to cleanse the federal government, among others, of the Red Menace? This committee wielded its subpoena power as a weapon and called citizens to testify in high-profile hearings. This intimidating atmosphere often produced dramatic but questionable revelations about communists infiltrating American institutions and subversive actions by well-known citizens, particularly in the political, sports and entertainment fields.

HUAC's controversial hearings contributed to the fear, distrust and repression that existed during the anticommunist hysteria of the 1950s. You remember Joseph McCarthy and his communist witch hunt during the infamous Red Scare? How many innocent lives were crushed by the arrogance and shamelessness of one United States senator, with help from HUAC?

Florida has its own sordid history of hysteria during this time. In the 1950s the Florida legislature created an investigation committee named the Johns Committee, after Sen. Charley Johns. This committee was in response to McCarthyism and the Red Scare; its purpose was to root out communists in suspect groups. When this effort fizzled, the committee chose a new target: gay and lesbian teachers and students in Florida's public schools and universities. Over the next four years, nearly 200 Florida teachers' and students' lives were changed forever.

It should be self-evident that neither McCarthyism and HUAC, nor the Johns Committee, were high moments in American history. In fact, they were embarrassing and tragic.

Think these two television shows were all fiction? Think that what is briefly described above following World War II can't happen again? Just the other day, Florida Sen. Rick Scott ranted at the liberal Democrat Party: "Today, we face the greatest danger we have ever faced: The militant left-wing in our country has become the enemy within. The woke Left now controls the Democrat Party. The entire federal government, the news media, academia, big tech, Hollywood, most corporate boardrooms, and now even some of our top military leaders... They want to end the American experiment. They want to replace freedom with control."

Never mind that the Departments of Justice (including the FBI) and Homeland Security have said the greatest domestic threat is posed by radical right-wing extremists. Scott echoes what many in his party truly believe: that he and his cohorts are making America great again and everyone who disagrees with them is the enemy.

Ah yes, a return to the glory days! This is what they want. You can hear their cry: down with the enemy! Let the investigations, witch hunts and character assassinations begin!

HOUSE OVERSIGHT AND FAIRNESS? HARDLY

Following the disclosures of government classified records at President Joe Biden's home and former office, the Republican-led House Oversight Committee is now demanding that President Biden turn over visitor logs of his Delaware home from the date of his inauguration to the present. In the words of Committee Chairman James Comer: "We have a lot of questions." The committee wants to find out who might have had access to classified documents and how the records got there.

Sounds fair enough. The committee wants to see if there are national security implications as a result of these documents possibly falling into the wrong hands.

Except for one thing.

No similar demand has been made of Donald Trump. The record is clear that Trump took hundreds of government records with him from the White House to his Mar-a-Lago home. We know Trump has had hundreds, perhaps thousands, of visitors to his estate, where he loves to show off his bounty and impress his audiences with his ostentatiousness. With classified records found throughout his estate, and some even off ground, the question of who had access and who might have inspected—or even carted off—records is a national security matter that must be answered in full.

To this day, we don't know why Trump took these records. One of his former lawyers opined that it was for leverage in the event Trump was indicted for his crimes. The belief is that he could exchange dismissal of any charges in return for these records.

A second possible reason is Trump has something to hide, and he needs those records to conceal information. We know how vigorously he resisted turning over any information or having to testify in any proceeding. His secretiveness belies his baseless claim of transparency.

But there is a third, far more disturbing, reason.

We also know that, over the years, Trump has cozied up to dictators and despots, like North Korea's Kim Jong Un, Turkey's Recep Tayyip Erdogen, China's Xi Jingping and Russia's Vladimir Putin, among others. We know how much Trump admires strength and abhors weakness; he admires—even envies—these men because of their strength, power and control over others. They demand unquestioned loyalty—just like Trump.

We also know how much Trump values money, because to him, money is power. We also know he's not as rich as he claims to be. Adding all this up, the question naturally arises whether Trump considered selling any of these records to one or more of these strongmen, or others for whatever reason.

Since Trump says he "did nothing wrong" when he called Ukraine's president seeking dirt on Biden's son in return for release of funds; when he urged his supporters to take the Capitol on January 6 to stop the lawful certification of the election; and when he stole those records, it's fair to wonder whether he planned to sell, or perhaps he's already sold, records to a fellow authoritarian.

His silly defense that he can declassify records "simply by thinking about it" only adds fuel to this fire. And since he believes he's incapable of breaking the law, if he did offer classified records for sale, he would think it perfectly proper, since he believes they're his records to do with as he pleases.

But we will never know any of this about Trump because the House Oversight Committee won't demand from Trump what they demand of Biden.

This utter failure to inquire of Trump the way it wants to inquire of Biden makes the House Committee's concern over national security a farce. This has nothing to do with national security; it has everything to do with raw politics. The message is clear: protect Trump at all costs; go after Biden at all costs.

This is also graphically demonstrated by House Judiciary Chairman Jim Jordan, who also announced an investigation into the discovery of these classified records. This election denier and certification obstructionist is now in charge of investigating the president he unsuccessfully prevented from taking office.

The evidence set out in the January 6 committee report overwhelmingly reveals that Jordan not only voted against certifying the 2020 presidential election results, but was "a significant player in President Trump's efforts" to overturn the election. Jordan "participated in numerous post-election meetings in which senior White House officials, Rudolph Giuliani, and others, discussed strategies for challenging the election, chief among them claims that the election had been tainted by fraud" despite all the evidence to the contrary.

The report says on "January 2, 2021, Representative Jordan led a conference call in which he, President Trump, and other Members of Congress discussed strategies for delaying the January 6th joint session." They also "discussed issuing social media posts encouraging President Trump's supporters to 'march to the Capitol' on the 6th." After that call on January 2, Jordan spoke to Trump for 18 minutes in a one-on-one phone conversation.

Also in the report: "Jordan texted Mark Meadows (Trump's chief of staff), passing along advice that Vice President (Mike) Pence should 'call out all the electoral votes that he believes are unconstitutional as no electoral votes at all.'"

The report cites other interactions between Jordan and Trump, including phone calls at least twice on January 6, 2021. Because Jordan made "inconsistent public statements about how many times they spoke and what they discussed" that day, his testimony before the committee became essential. However, Jordan refused to comply with the committee's subpoena.

Just before the bipartisan committee was shut down by the incoming Republican leadership, it referred Jordan, as well as other Republicans who defied subpoenas including House Speaker Kevin McCarthy, to the House Ethics Committee. The January 6 committee concluded that if "left unpunished," it "undermines Congress's longstanding power to investigate in support of its lawmaking authority."

Instead of following up on the committee's ethics referrals, the House Republican Steering Committee that chooses committee chairs instead elevated Jordan to chairman of the Judiciary Committee.

As with the House Oversight Committee, Jordan's message is clear: protect Trump at all costs; go after Biden at all costs.

A PRIMER ON GOVERNMENT RECORDS, CLASSIFIED OR NOT

With all the brouhaha over classified records involving former President Trump and President Biden, it's worth briefly looking into federal law that deals with government records, whether classified or not.

There are three laws cited in connection with Trump's records. The search warrant gave prosecutors the right to seize records at his estate for evidence of violations of (for non-lawyers, USC stands for United States Code, where all federal laws are codified):

18 USC Sec. 793, which prevents unauthorized possession of national defense information. The failure to keep national defense information safe is punishable by up to 10 years in prison. This law was initially passed under the 1917 Espionage Act, which predates the current statutory classification system.

18 USC Sec. 1519, deals with destruction, alteration, or falsification of records in federal investigations; and

18 USC Sec. 2071, regarding concealment, removal, or mutilation generally.

The latter two laws make it illegal to conceal or destroy official federal government documents. They are punishable by up to three and 20 years in prison, respectively.

What is important here is that neither of these three laws has any bearing on whether the records involved are classified or not.

Federal law makes it illegal to intentionally take classified documents to an unauthorized location, but that law was not among the three cited in the Trump search warrant. This means that whether or not the documents seized from Trump's estate were classified has no bearing on these three charges.

The laws that deal with intentional disclosure, removal and retention of classified information are:

18 U.S. Code § 798, which prohibits knowingly and willfully disclosing classified information to an unauthorized person, etc.; and

18 USC Sec. 1924, which prohibits unauthorized removal and retention of classified information.

Ironically, Trump in 2018 signed a change in the law which increased the maximum prison term for individuals convicted of mishandling classified information from one to five years.

Two of these laws are noteworthy because they were frequently cited after the disclosure in 2016 that Hillary Clinton used a private email server for official public communications rather than using official State Department email accounts maintained on federal servers. Those two laws are sections 793 and 1924. Both laws require proof of intent. Even though the Justice Department was under Trump's control for four years, and charges could have been brought against her at any time during those years, she was never charged. Presumably, the reason is there was no proof of criminal intent.

There is yet another law.

In 1978, Congress passed the Presidential Records Act, which provides that any records created or received by the President as part of his constitutional, statutory, or ceremonial duties are the property of the United States government and will be managed by National Archives at the end of the administration. This law was in response to Watergate; specifically to President Richard Nixon's intent to destroy records relating to his presidential tenure upon his resignation in 1974.

Note this law governs the official records of presidents and vice presidents that were made or received after January 20, 1981 (beginning with the Reagan Administration). This law changed the legal ownership of the official records of the president from private to public, and established a new statutory structure under which presidents, and the archives, must manage the records of their administrations.

FOR THE REPUBLICAN WHATABOUTERS

It seems that whenever a Republican official or candidate is called out for wrongdoing, the party faithful respond by saying the Democrats are no different. It's called "whataboutism" and it's now being played loud and clear by Donald Trump's supporters over the discovery of classified records in Joe Biden's former office and at his Delaware residence.

That the facts are different means nothing to the whatabouters. Fact: Biden didn't take boxes with hundreds of classified documents and stash them around his estate. Fact: Biden hasn't claimed he declassified these records by "thinking about it." Fact: Biden had the records turned over to the archives the day after they were discovered. Trump had to be subpoenaed because he lied when he was originally asked to return all records he took from the White House. Fact: Trump intended to take those records, saying to this day, he did "nothing wrong." There is no evidence that Biden intended to remove classified records.

There are certainly significant factual differences, whether the whatabouters admit them or not.

But there are so many more.

When Al Gore lost the 2000 presidential election, he didn't claim the election was "rigged" or stolen from him by voter fraud. After the courts disposed of all cases, he accepted the loss in the interest of uniting the nation.

Gore didn't knowingly and repeatedly lie about a stolen election. He didn't light the flame for an attack on the nation's capital that resulted in multiple deaths and destruction of property. He didn't try to stop the constitutionally mandated certification of electoral college results.

We all know what Trump did when he lost in 2020. No Democrat ever did that.

Let's take a look at some of the current House members for more false examples of whataboutism.

Election denier and Trump loyalist Marjorie Taylor Greene was removed from committee assignments in the last Congress for her racist comments and antisemitic conspiracy theories, and for encouraging violence against Democrats. She was booted off committees for her disgraceful comments. House Speaker Kevin McCarthy nevertheless rewarded her with appointments to the Homeland Security Committee and the House Oversight Committee.

To the whatabouters out there, give me the name of a Democrat House member who made racial and antisemitic comments and was rewarded with appointment to a House committee.

The Homeland Security Committee is usually made up of representatives with military or intelligence experience; Greene has neither. What she does have are wacky conspiracy theories and extreme fealty to Trump and McCarthy.

The oversight committee handles investigations and has become a home for far right members to go after the Biden administration. In addition to Greene, it now includes Lauren Boebert, Scott Perry, Byron Donalds, and Gary Palmer, all of whom are Trump loyalists and election deniers.

For these folks, ideology and loyalty trump qualifications and competence for their committee assignments.

Hey whatabouters, how many Democrat representatives are there who are election deniers from 2016--or from any presidential election, for that matter? How many Democrats fueled violence over election results, and tried to stop the constitutional certification process from going forward?

Representative Paul Gosar was removed from committees two years ago after threatening Democrat lawmakers on social media. McCarthy rewarded him by putting him back on the Natural Resources committee, and also put him on the Oversight Committee.

Whatabouters, how many Democrat representatives threatened Republican lawmakers on social media and were rewarded with House committee appointments?

Rep. George Santos has serious trouble with the truth. He's lied about every facet of his life—parents, childhood, education, employment—even his name. Yet, he remains in Congress solely because McCarthy can't afford to lose any more party members. (Whether Santos remains in Congress for his full term is iffy. Santos is facing pressure to resign as his campaign lies appear to include shady financing.)

Ok, whatabouters, identify a Democrat member of Congress with anything close to Santos' history of deceit.

Just the other day, it was reported that an unsuccessful Republican candidate for state office in New Mexico who attributed his defeat to a "rigged" election stands accused of masterminding a series of shootings targeting the homes of elected Democrats.

Never mind the absence of any outrage from Republican officials; and never mind the obvious danger of violence inherent in false claims of a "rigged" election; when has a Democrat candidate made the same false claim and followed up by masterminding shootings into the homes of elected Republicans?

Whatabouters are certainly entitled to their opinions, however unmoored from objective reality they may be. However, they are not entitled to their facts.

THE REPUBLICAN PARTY'S MOMENT OF TRUTH IS FAST APPROACHING

With Donald Trump's blast at evangelical leaders for not backing his 2024 presidential run, the Republican Party is rapidly approaching the crossroads. The party leaders must decide whether to disavow him as a candidate and effectively dump him now, or hope against hope that events between now and next year result in his undoing.

Now that Trump has attacked the leadership of the party's strongest group of supporters, party leaders who rely on the evangelical vote must come to a decision about Trump. Kevin McCarthy, Jim Jordan, Margorie Taylor Greene, etc., in the House; Ted Cruz, Lindsey Graham, Josh Hawley, etc. in the Senate all must find the brains, heart and most of all courage to tell Trump in no uncertain terms that his time as a party leader has come and gone. The disavowal and dumping must be swift, certain and complete.

Here's why.

The latter choice—letting events make that decision--is a dicey one at best. Even after two impeachments; his incompetent handling of the COVID pandemic; all the revelations from January 6; and his removal of classified documents from the White House, he still retains a sizeable base of support among Republicans---mostly from the right wing that includes evangelicals. His infamous line that he could shoot someone and still have millions of supporters is a sad, but true, statement.

But here's something else that's true. He has never won the popular vote. In his two campaigns for president, he lost the popular vote to Hillary Clinton by 2.9 million in 2016 and to Joe Biden by 7 million in 2020. Clinton won the popular vote even with extensive baggage of her own making. Biden won before the public knew of January 6's lies and violence, and the confidential records fiasco, all of Trump's own making.

If Biden is the Democrat nominee, however his confidential records mess turns out will be of no import if Trump is the nominee because his situation is far more profound. In sum, Trump has no advantage here.

If Biden chooses not to run, however, a nominee such as Govs. Gretchen Whitmer of Michigan, J. K. Pritzker of Illinois, or Gavin Newsome of California, or any number of Democrat governors or senators, would be most formidable. Each would be favored over Trump because none would have the baggage Trump has.

In fact, no candidate from either party—no matter who it might be–would have Trump's baggage. Trump can't depend on getting broad Republican support; in fact, he can't depend on getting the same level of Republican support he's gotten in the past.

Does anyone in the Republican Party seriously believe Trump, after all we now know about him, would get more popular votes in 2024 than he did in 2016 and 2020?

If it wasn't absolutely clear before, it certainly is now: Trump is all about loyalty to him. Anyone who voices disagreement with him or shows anything other than complete loyalty is added to his increasingly lengthy hit list. He has no loyalty to party or person. If he's not neutralized as a candidate sooner rather than later, he will pick up his marbles and either run as a third party candidate or do what he did in Georgia—tell his base to sit out the election because without him in it, the election is rigged--a fraud, etc. His intransigence in Georgia helped elected a Democrat. If he's not removed from consideration this year, he will take the Republican Party down with him next year. Trump simply doesn't care about the Republican Party. For him, the party was his vehicle to get into the White House. He has no principles or conscience; he will try to destroy anyone who runs against him.

As soon as the McCarthys and Cruzes get it in their heads that Trump is a loser in 2024 and is willing to sacrifice the party if he's not the nominee, the better for their party's chances next year.

The party leaders would be wise to dump him now and make it clear to their base that he's history and the future of the party is found in such leaders as (insert names here).

The longer Trump is in the picture, the better it is for the Democrats.

Sadly, there isn't much wisdom in today's Republican Party. And not a lot of brains, heart or courage, either.

Which suits the Democrats just fine.

"IGNORANCE IS BLISS"

This is a rather common phrase most, if not all, of us have heard at one time or another. Considering the current state of education in conservative states, this has taken on greater significance.

This phrase comes from a line from Thomas Gray's poem, Ode on a Distant Prospect at Eton College: "Where ignorance is bliss, Tis folly to be wise." The shortened version "ignorance is bliss" can be taken to be an excuse to be lazy of mind and therefore be happier.

This phrase has positive and negative connotations. In some ways, ignorance is bliss when certain things are beyond our control. On the other hand, ignoring actual problems of direct impact can lead to snowballing consequences.

There is another aspect to this quote: Knowledge is power and ignorance is bliss, so the saying goes. This means that knowing what is going on and becoming aware is far superior to being blissfully ignorant; in short, if you don't know about something, you don't worry about it—and you can't worry about it.

When it comes to historical events, if you don't know it, it didn't happen. It doesn't mean these events didn't happen; it just means you don't know they happened. And if you don't know they happened, then it's impossible to learn the lessons taught by those events. Recall another saying: those who fail to learn the lessons of history are condemned to repeat them.

Over the past few years, there have been repeated assaults on academic freedom from the right wing, not only here in Florida but in other red states as well. This assault is directed at all levels of education—elementary, secondary and college. The most recent example is Tallahassee Community College, where its president joined the other Florida College System (FCS) presidents in cowering to Gov. Ron DeSantis's cleansing of curriculum.

Here is a key part of what the FCS presidents said:

"As such, our institutions will not fund or support any institutional practice, policy, or academic requirement that compels belief in critical race theory or related concepts such as intersectionality, or the idea that systems of oppression should be the primary lens through which teaching and learning are analyzed and/or improved upon...."

It is noted that TCC doesn't have any critical race theory program or activity, and has no employee with diversity, equity and inclusion in the title or job description. In fact, there isn't a single educational institution in Florida that teaches critical race theory. Thus, the governor and legislature banned a subject not taught in this state.

But that doesn't matter because it's all about keeping the base happy, and if they believe something is being taught that shouldn't be, that's all that matters. Fire them up and keep them angry; that's the message.

It is further noted that TCC did inform the state Department of Education that "If CRT is discussed by students on campus it is subject to civil debate and discussion, just like any other theory or topic within the academic environment, to allow students freedom to form their own opinions." Thus, while students can discuss forbidden subjects on their own, they won't be a part of any curriculum or formal study, even though they're only theories.

There are several slippery slopes here. First, what exactly is critical race theory? What it means to some might not be in sync with the views of others. Second, when does a course of study meet someone's definition of "intersectionality," or "that systems of oppression should be the primary lens" of instruction?

Third, and most important, this curriculum cleansing doesn't only apply to these matters, however they're defined by the government censors.

GEORGE WAAS

Recall that legislation to eliminate woke instruction included any matter that causes psychological distress or discomfort. Webster defines "woke" as being aware of and actively attentive to important societal facts and issues (especially issues of racial and social justice). Thus, subjects or courses of study that raises awareness of and active attention to important facts and issues, especially those pertaining to racial and social justice, that makes people feel uncomfortable are targets for removal.

What other studies might make students uncomfortable or cause distress? Teaching about the Holocaust? What about World War I when the Germans sank American ships? Or World War II when Japan bombed Pearl Harbor? How about 9/11 when Arabs drove planes into the Twin Towers and the Pentagon? The point here is that each of these subjects—and so many others—will cause some distress and discomfort.

In fact, history is replete with distressful and uncomfortable—and tragic—events that must be taught, lest we forget.

By way of example, if World War II is taught from the perspective that America was attacked but eventually won the war and everyone lived happily ever after, that's not teaching; that's indoctrination. Teaching a sanitized version of history, civics, social studies, and related subjects, by glossing over or removing those items critical to the learning process solely to avoid unpleasantness is

208

classic indoctrination. Teaching the unvarnished truth is not indoctrination; teaching falsehoods solely to avoid the truth is.

History is the great teacher of behavior to avoid in the future. If future generations aren't taught history's tragic events like war, the Holocaust—man's inhumanity to man—how do future generations know what to avoid? Without this knowledge, there is repetition.

The FCS presidents, in their memo, said they "remain committed to developing campus environments that uphold objectivity in teaching and learning and in professional development and that welcome all voices — environments in which students, faculty, and staff can pursue their academic interests without fear of reprisal or being "canceled." Uh huh. Sure.

Teaching our young to think critically evidently isn't part of the current cleansing plan.

What is the opposite of woke? Ignorance. Blissful ignorance.

A SOBERING THOUGHT

My wife and I just returned home from a three-week visit to the Middle East. Along with another couple, we flew to Israel and met up with about 70 others for a visit to Israel, Egypt and Jordan. We spent five days in Israel, five in

Egypt and five in Jordan, before wrapping up our journey with six days in Jerusalem.

In both Egypt and Jordan, we barely had time to visit the key sites; nevertheless, there was one thing that was quite obvious: the level of security. In Egypt, our bus caravan was guarded in front, back on and both sides by armed security guards. Areas around the pyramids and the Sphinx were also under armed guard.

The main sites we saw in Jordan—the stark desert of Wadi Rum, the mountain city of Petra—were also under guard, only not as overt as in Egypt.

Then there were the frequent security checkpoints—dogs sniffing our buses, guards examining under the buses for explosives—and, for our flight in Egypt from our ship in the Suez Canal to Luxor and the Valley of Kings, we had to go through multiple personal searches—removing shoes, belts, name tags, emptying all pockets, etc.

It is an understatement to say that security and safety are of paramount importance in this the hottest of flashpoints in the world.

But we observed the real extent of security measures in the Middle East when we were in Jerusalem. First, it is a misperception that Jerusalem is a small city. To be sure, the old city where the three great religions meet, and where history and religion meet, is small—about one square mile.

But outside of the wall that surrounds ancient Jerusalem, there lies a big modern metropolitan city.

We noticed Muslims and Jews living side by side, mingling and just going about their business.

In the old city, however, security is at its most intense. Remember all of these significant religious sites—The Western Wall, Church of the Holy Sepulchre, Temple Mount, Dome of the Rock—are literally next to one another. We were not allowed to visit the Dome of the Rock, which is under Arab control. The several entrances were strongly guarded, although one guard actually acknowledged and winked at me.

The most significant presence of security was the time we visited what is called "The Market;" streets some as long as a football field lined with shops on both sides. Thousands of people in a party atmosphere dancing, singing, celebrating, and selling food and trinkets, with uniformed armed guards frequently interspersed among the boisterous throng.

But something else struck me. There was absolutely no demonstration of fear of attack. I never saw anyone show any concern anywhere for their safety or wellbeing. Shootings, when they occur over there, are committed by radical extremists, not random shooters looking to settle some private score.

There is a reason for this.

In Israel, No one may own or carry a gun without showing a reason to do so. A special permit by the interior ministry is then required. The permit must have the approval of the police and includes information about the owner and the gun type. With a population of about 8.5 million, about 135,000 citizens are currently licensed to own guns. Of those, 37,500 work as guards, according to the Ministry of Public Security, which issues the permits.

In Egypt, the gun laws prohibit any civilian from carrying a firearm in public. Guns are allowed only for specific licensed personnel. To get a gun possession permit, the applicant must apply to the chief of security in one's district and province. It is the Ministry of Interior that issues a gun or firearm permit.

Jordan also has strict gun laws, requiring licensure and training to own a handgun. It is illegal to own an automatic weapon.

Where guns are permitted, there is a limit on the number of bullets that can be purchases.

There is, however, another reason. If someone is hellbent on launching an attack, he must be willing to give up his life as well as those who will be killed in a retaliatory attack that will most assuredly come in a matter of days, if not hours.

While we were in the Middle East, violence flared up in and around both the Gaza Strip and the West Bank. The perpetrators were quickly disposed of, and there was swift retaliation.

During that same period of time that we were in the Middle East, however, there were 30 mass shootings here, costing the lives of 51 innocent law-abiding people, with dozens more injured.

Of course, our population of 335 million far exceeds the total population of all three countries. But these three countries don't have the random mass shootings we have, and the population variance doesn't justify or provide any comfort for the number of random mass shootings that occur here, and undoubtedly will continue to occur here.

We have a gun problem here, and laws allowing one to purchase a gun without a permit or training under the "constitutional carry" rubric will only add to the problem.

Our problem is driven by too many guns; too much emphasis on guns; laws making it easier and easier to get guns; too much politically driven anger, resentment and hatred; and too many nuts with real or imaginary scores to settle.

The stated purpose of these gun laws is to protect the rights of the law-abiding people. Under our system of justice, however, everyone is presumed to be law-abiding until they are charged, tried and convicted of a crime. Someone who's law-abiding when he gets his hands on a weapon but chooses to settle a score becomes a criminal too late in this process. Innocent lives are needlessly lost at the hands of this former law-abiding citizen.

(Notice, however, that these gun laws don't apply to those places where government decisions are made. Evidently it's perfectly ok to carry a gun into a mall or supermarket but not in a courthouse or government office building. Can't run the risk of an angered person carrying a gun into a legislative chamber, courtroom, or governor's office; it's perfectly fine if that angry person takes his weapon into a mall or shopping center.)

Another reason given is self-defense. The instances where a person uses a weapon to confront a legitimate threat to his life amount to about 2% of all instances. Further, the question can be asked what exactly is meant by self-defense. A fired employee who believes he's been wronged decides to defend his honor and integrity by seeking revenge. A student who receives a failing grade and is mocked by his peers decides he must defend his honor and integrity by getting back at his teacher and fellow students. Surely, in their mind, they are acting in self-defense. Hatred, by any means, can provoke one to believe in destroying "the enemy" as a means of defending himself and his kind.

To the sane and rational, this is nonsense; the act of a crazed person. But remember, we are not dealing with rational people here; but until they act out their anger and resentment, they are deemed law-abiding citizens entitled to the full protection of the law.

As for constitutional rights, do these government officials consider the constitutional rights of innocent victims of these acts of violence? What about their constitutional right to life, liberty and the pursuit of happiness? What about their right to live in a safe, secure environment? No word from the "constitutional carry" advocates about these rights.

A third reason is collection. People are collectors, and gun collections are nothing new. But who collects assault weapons? How many display to family, friends and associates their collection of assault rifles? How many proudly tell their employers and co-workers of their bountiful collection of AR-15s?

Putting it bluntly, the "constitutional carry" advocates long for the days of the wild west, fancying themselves as modern-day John Waynes, Clint Eastwoods, etc. Gun ownership is viewed as a measure of masculinity and power.

But with a population of 335 million, and an adult population of 270 million, there are 400 million guns on the street in our country. That's 110 million more guns than cars. This is a dangerous oversaturation of lethal weapons and diminution of the responsibility that goes with being a gun owner.

For all professions, occupations and businesses, a license of some type is required. This is vital in order for the public to ascertain minimal competence. A license is required to drive a car. There are other examples of license requirements to show minimal competence. For those who foolishly equate death by automobile with gun deaths, remember that the primary purpose of a car is for transportation; the primary purpose of a firearm is to shoot.

Perhaps these countries, as well as others who have enacted common sense gun laws, know something we've lost sight of. In any event, purchasing a gun should be more difficult than buying a loaf of bread or container of milk.

THE LATEST TO PRACTICE THE ART OF DEFLECTION AND DELAY: MIKE PENCE

Once again, Republicans at the top embark on a delay and distract strategy. The latest is former VP Mike Pence who plans to object to a special counsel subpoena into January 6, relying on the Constitution's "speech and debate" clause that generally shields members of Congress from testifying about legislative matters. His objection will meet his former boss Donald Trump's objection to the same subpoena on grounds of executive privilege.

This is another frivolous, bogus effort to block the search for the truth and accountability. Pence was not a member of Congress on January 6. He was elected as part of the executive branch. He is not a legislator. As president of the Senate, he votes only when there's a tie. The special counsel's subpoena has nothing to do with legislative activities; it has everything to do with communications between him and Trump before the January 6 attack on the capital when they were vice president and president, respectively. Further, the "speech and debate" clause can't be used to shield criminal activity, which is precisely the subject of the subpoena.

As for Trump's executive privilege claim, he has tried this one before and failed. The courts have told him this privilege can't be used to avoid inquiry into criminal matters. Of course, previous court decisions wouldn't stop him from relying on the same baseless tactic. No one really believes he would adhere to prior court rulings. When above the law, proceed accordingly. He still professes his feckless belief in a rigged election....and as long as millions are willing to buy his repeated lies, he'll keep repeating them ad nauseam.

We can expect the party mouthpieces to claim Pence and Trump are being transparent; they just want to protect constitutional rights. Again, as long as millions believe this nonsense, they will repeat that lame refrain over and over again.

Boxing legend Joe Louis, talking about an opponent's strategy, famously said "he can run, but he can't hide." A most appropriate quote to describe the latest effort at deflection.

THERE IS NOTHING WRONG WITH TEACHING THEORIES AS THEORIES. THIS IS DONE EVERY DAY

With all the brouhaha over book-banning and curriculum cleansing, one point stands out: what is wrong with teaching theories? Specifically, what is wrong with teaching critical race theory as one theory? Theories are taught in our education institutions every day. A theory is not fact; if it were, it would be so labeled.

A theory is a belief, policy, or procedure proposed or followed as the basis of action; an ideal or hypothetical set of facts, principles, or circumstances; a hypothesis assumed for the sake of argument or investigation.

Examples abound. There are five primary educational learning theories: behaviorism, cognitive, constructivism, humanism, and connectivism.

The theories of teaching science include: learning theory, science education, behaviorism, cognitivism, constructivism, mastery learning, acquisition of knowledge, and remedial education.

Astronomy has the Big Bang Theory. Biology has the Cell Theory. There is the Theory of Evolution; the Germ Theory of Disease. Chemistry has the Atomic Theory and the Kinetic Theory of Gases. Physics has the Theory of Relativity; and on and on.

Mathematical theories include Algebraic K-theory, Almgren–Pitts min-max theory, Approximation theory, Bifurcation theory and the Brill–Noether theory.

The point here is that theories are part of the curriculum in our schools. Each of these, and many others, are taught in schools across the country every day with no concern whatever. So, what is so harmful or dangerous to conservatives in teaching critical race theory as just that; a theory, just like so many other theories? The answer is blame or accountability. Critical race theory proceeds from the view that racial bias is inherent in many parts of western society, especially in its legal and social institutions, on the basis of their having been primarily designed for and implemented by white people.

Because some government leaders on the right believe this is untrue, they don't want it taught in their school systems. They have decided for the rest of us what is true and capable of being taught, and what is untrue and must be banned. The problem with this line of thinking should be obvious: at what point does it end? If they can decide truth for themselves and foist that on the public, they take away the thinking and learning of the masses that is critical to the survival of a Democracy.

Well, they may be right in their view that critical race theory is false; but they may also be wrong. And this applies equally to any theory. One day, a particular theory may be proven right or wrong. We learn and we move on. We learn more and more about our world and nation every day. What we believed to be true or false years ago has, upon further investigation, been proven to be the opposite.

Having been overseas and witnessing the degree of archeological searches in these ancient lands, I have no doubt that things we believe as fact today will be disproven tomorrow.

With specific regard to critical race theory, a few years ago, Richard Rothstein, a leading authority on housing policy, questioned the notion that America's cities came to be racially divided through de facto segregation--that is, through individual prejudices, income differences, or the actions of private institutions like banks and real estate agencies. Rather, his book, The Color of Law, makes the case that it was de jure segregation--the laws and policy decisions passed by local, state, and federal governments--that actually promoted the discriminatory patterns that continue to this day.

He argues that there was an overwhelming amount of government policy at the state, local and federal level that explicitly forced black people to live in different places from white people through zoning and redlining.

In the United States, redlining is a discriminatory practice in which services are withheld from potential customers who reside in neighborhoods classified as "hazardous" to investment; these neighborhoods have significant numbers of racial and ethnic minorities, and low-income residents.

We are certainly familiar with Jim Crow laws, and a few Supreme Court decisions. that give relevance to this theory, so why not allow for teaching critical race theory that addresses zoning, redlining, Jim Crow, court decisions, and the civil rights movement? Even if Rothstein's theory has a scintilla of merit; even if both de facto and de jure segregation influenced race relations to some small measure, what is wrong with teaching these points as theories deserving of further examination to see if they prove to be true or false? Why allow government officials to effectively think for us and cut off lines of educational inquiry?

We learn from inquiry spurred on by curiosity. Why shut off avenues of education solely because someone's feelings might be hurt? The search for truth can be painful; it will also lead to better educated citizens and better decisions going forward.

While books can be kept out of the school system, they can't be removed from the libraries and Internet. Let students read what's out there: theory, fiction, history, etc., and let them discuss with others and make their own judgments. After all, this is what education is all about.

PENCE HAS A ROUGH ROAD AHEAD IN TRYING TO AVOID A DOJ SUBPOENA FOR HIS TESTIMONY ON JANUARY 6

Former VP Mike Pence has vowed to fight the DOJ special counsel's subpoena for evidence pertaining to the investigation into former President Donald Trump's actions surrounding the January 6 attack on the nation's capital.

He has called the demand for his cooperation "unprecedented and unconstitutional."

"No vice president has ever been subject to a subpoena to testify about the president with whom they served," Pence said.

What he says is absolutely true. However, it is also absolutely true that what Trump did is unprecedented and unconstitutional. No president has ever behaved the way Trump did both in public and as reported in numerous articles and books since that fateful day. His demand of his vice president to act unconstitutionally and reject the Electoral College results is part of the broad criminal investigation now in the hands of the DOJ special counsel.

Pence has vowed to take his fight to the Supreme Court if necessary. This is certainly welcome news to Trump, as one effect of his stonewalling will be to delay his testimony well into next year at the earliest, giving his former boss time to run his campaign for a return trip to the White House. Recall that Trump was willing to put Pence's life in jeopardy in order to illegally remain in office. Apparently, the courage Pence showed on January 6 has crumbled along with his backbone.

Pence intends to rely on a unique, unprecedented legal strategy that he's immune from testifying because of legal protections for members of Congress, because he was acting as president of the Senate during the January 6 Electoral College vote certification rather than as a member of the executive branch.

"For me, this is a moment where you have to decide where you stand, and I stand on the Constitution of the United States," Pence said.

Setting aside his moral indignation, whether feigned or legitimate, at the government's audacity of compelling him to offer evidence under oath in a criminal investigation just like every other citizen who has relevant evidence, let's look at the merits of his claim that he was functioning as a legislator rather than as the second highest official in the executive branch of the federal government.

Pence is relying on the "Speech and Debate" clause contained in Article 1, section 6, of the Constitution, which says that "for any Speech or Debate in either House, they [members] shall not be questioned in any other Place."

The general purpose of the speech and debate clause is to protect members of Congress from having to worry that anything they say in the course of legislative activities will implicate them in a lawsuit. It is well-established that asking a legislator why he or she proposed a bill or how he or she voted on a piece of legislation is off limits. Inquiry into a legislator's motivations or mental impressions is forbidden.

In United States v. Brewster, the Supreme Court distinguished between "purely legislative activities," which the Speech and Debate Clause protected, and merely political activities, which it did not. The Supreme Court made it clear that the Speech or Debate Clause protects against inquiry into acts that occur in the regular course of the legislative process and into the motivation for those acts.

Legislative action has been defined as the development, drafting, introduction, consideration, modification, adoption, rejection, review, enactment or defeat of any bill, resolution, amendment, report, nomination, proposed administrative rule or other matter by the legislature or by either house or any committee, subcommittee, joint or select committee thereof, or by a legislator or employee of the legislature acting in an official capacity.

From this, the question becomes whether Pence's action, which he admits is ministerial in certifying the Electoral College results, is one that occurs in the ordinary course of the legislative process and involves inquiry into his motivation for that action.

Ministerial certification of Electoral College results is not an act that occurs in the regular course of legislative activities. This singular act meets none of the items listed in the definition of legislative action. It is not an act of the Congress and it doesn't involve inquiry into a legislator's mental impressions or mindset behind his or her vote on a legislative item. Indeed, because this particular certification is a ministerial act, there is no mental impression or motive involved.

Pence is not a member of Congress. He's not a legislator. He takes part in no legislative process or debate. His name doesn't appear on any proposed or adopted legislation. He votes only to break a tie. In fact, if he did participate in any activity except breaking tie votes. serving as presiding officer in the Senate and certifying Electoral College results, there would be a clear separation of powers issue that a sitting vice president, as part of the top executive team, would be injecting his role into the legislative process. That's a clear no-no.

Up against Pence's extremely weak argument on the Speech and Debate Clause is the Supreme Court's oft-repeated position that "the public has a right to every man's evidence." Branzburg v. Hayes, 408 U.S. 665 (1972). You may recall Richard Nixon tried to block access to his tapes of office conversations the disclosure of which led to his resignation. In that case, the Court reiterated this principle of the public's "right to every man's evidence."

In the DOJ special counsel's investigation, he is representing the people in determining whether the evidence gathered is sufficient to bring criminal charges against Trump and others. If charges are filed against the ex-president, the case will read "The United States v. Donald J. Trump."

Pence may well be hoping for a favorable audience from the Supreme Court's six-member conservative bloc. Trump of course had this same wish before the Court ruled against him in his "rigged election" and other feckless claims.

It would be wise for Pence's lawyers to be paid a handsome retainer up front.

PARTIAL GEORGIA GRAND JURY REPORT FULL OF SOUND AND FURY, YET SIGNIFIES NOTHING

The Fulton County, Georgia, grand jury has issued its long-awaited report on shenanigans involving the 2020 presidential election; specifically Donald Trump's efforts to have Georgia election officials "find" more than 11,000 votes needed to overturn the official vote totals to win that state's electoral college votes.

There is an old Greek proverb that says: "The mountain that labored and brought forth a mouse." This refers to great promises and great labors that produce little results.

Such is the case here...so far. The grand jury made two findings. First, it concluded unanimously that there was no widespread voter fraud. No surprise here.

Next, it concluded that one or more witnesses may have committed perjury in their testimony; that is, they lied under oath on matters material to the investigation. Nothing new here, either.

Lying has been at the core of the Republican Party for the past several years. In fact, it was a lie that led to the January 6 riot at the capital, and it's that lie too many members of Congress bought into that plagues us to this day.

The grand jury is urging the state prosecutors to file perjury charges "where the evidence is compelling." I thought the grand jury considered this point in its investigation.

While this report may be full of sound and fury, it signifies nothing. However, it is hoped that the day of accountability for the scofflaws will come sooner rather than later. This recalls another quote: "Justice delayed is justice denied."

A SAD COMMENTARY ON THE RIGHT WING'S MOST LOYAL AUDIENCE

One of the main conclusions of the House January 6 Investigating Committee is that ex-president Donald Trump knew he lost the 2020 election, yet nevertheless pressed his Big Lie that the election was rigged, stolen from him, and that he really won. This lie led to a riot at the capital that cost the loss of several lives and damaged the great symbol of our Democracy.

Hundreds are now in jail because they believed Trump's lie to such an extent that they were willing to do violence in his name. To this day, there are still those who stand ready to engage in violence on his behalf, even in the absence of any evidence to support Trump's claims.

Now comes the revelation that one of the most ardent Trump supporters, Fox News, knew Trump's claim of a rigged election was false, yet its employees involved in election coverage knew that the election wasn't stolen and that his many fraud claims were false. This revelation comes in the form of a court filing that is part of an ongoing defamation lawsuit filed against the network by Dominion Voting Systems. Fox News commentators repeatedly falsely claimed Dominion rigged the election machinery to favor Joe Biden.

This filing includes comments and quotes revealing that producers, executives and stars of the network knew that Trump's claims were bogus, yet were repeated again and again on air as a way to boost ratings and appease Fox's conservative viewers, who executives feared were abandoning the channel for other conservative media outlets.

Specifically, major Fox News commentators Sean Hannity and Tucker Carlson said in private that they knew that Trump lawyer Sidney Powell, who filed election lawsuits to stop multiple states that Joe Biden had won from certifying their elections, was not telling the truth.

"That whole narrative that Sidney was pushing, I did not believe it for one second," Hannity said, according to the legal filing.

The evidence that Trump knew he was pushing a lie, now coupled with Fox News privately dismissed Trump's bogus claims of voter fraud even as the network's top stars repeated them on TV, says a lot about how Trump views his supporters and how Fox News network executives and commentators view their audience.

And it's not a positive take on their most loyal and supportive advocates.

Trump once famously said he "could stand in the middle of Fifth Avenue (in New York) and shoot somebody, and I wouldn't lose any voters." Sadly, he is right. His support among rigid loyalists is so strong he simply can do no wrong in their eyes.

But what he did, and now what Fox New did, was to take that strong base of loyalty and turn it on its head.

Putting it bluntly, these loyalists were played, and they willingly let themselves be played.

Trump and Fox News must view their diehard supporters with such disdain that they can say and do anything, yet their rock-ribbed base will be there for them no matter what.

They have to believe their audience is gullible, easily swayed, perhaps ignorant and maybe even stupid enough to blindly accept whatever BS they dish out.

To be sure, Trump has lost some of his supporters, as has Fox News, but it's the size of what remains that is most important to them, and most disconcerting for everyone else.

Some commentators have opined that it's time for a reality check for those who still follow Trump, and by extension, Fox News.

It took master con artists to play their audience so successfully for so long.

It's hard for anyone to admit they've been taken advantage of; that they've been suckered into something so damning and embarrassing that they must be called upon to question their own judgment.

Realizing a mistake and rectifying it takes strength and courage. It's ok to make mistakes; that's what makes us human. No human being is perfect, not even Donald Trump (although he acts as if he believes he is.)

If we make a mistake, we fess up to it and we move on, hoping to learn from the error of our ways. That's called growth through education. We learn more from our mistakes than our successes.

Following Trump, and taking as true everything Fox News dishes out, are losing propositions. The Republican Party has better candidates than Trump, and there are news outlets far more reliable than Fox News.

CNN fired Chris Cuomo for aiding his brother, then-New York

Gov. Andrew Cuomo, in connection with the latter's sexual harassment issues that eventually forced the governor to resign. Cuomo's journalistic failure is far less consequential than what Hannity, Carlson and others did at Fox in support of Trump, yet so far neither has faced accountability for their repeated waxing of Trump's lies even as they knew better.

We will see if Fox News has any journalistic integrity left after this latest and most glaring embarrassment.

There is no fault for those who followed Trump and Fox News but who now see the error of their ways by placing their faith in false prophets. Having visited churches here, in Europe and the Middle East, I've seen the awesome power of faith and its essential vitality in peoples' lives.

We want to believe in our elected public officials. We want to believe what news reporters and commentators tell us. Our entire system of government ultimately runs on faith.

But there are those who take advantage of this knowledge and use peoples' faith as a vehicle for personal success regardless of the costs. They will lie, cheat and steal from those who placed their faith in them.

Meanwhile, for the millions who still blindly support Trump after all the revelations about him and his overt aberrant conduct, and for those who still believe what Fox News dishes out night after night, what is to be said about them?

Are they intelligent, knowledgeable, educated critical thinkers and analysts, or simply malleable, blind cultists who without question accept whatever they dish out, like putty in the hands of a master craftsman?

REPUBLICANS COULD LEARN A FEW LESSONS

Going forward toward 2024, the Republican Party could learn a few lessons about what won't work for them. The party leaders have already been given ample notice and warning: the red wave expected in the House last year never materialized, and Michigan changed from majority Republican to majority Democrat in 2022.

Here are a few of the lessons the party needs to learn.

First, they must cut the conspiracy theories.

No more Pizzagates. No more Q'Anon. No more vaccine refusal based on conspiracy nonsense, such as the unproven link between vaccines and autism. No more Area 51 alien silliness. No more "deep state" rubbish. No more of Sarah

Palin-like "death panels." No more baseless JFK, Malcolm X and Martin Luther King assassination theories. No more "stop the steal" madness. No more Dominion voting machines being rigged as part of an international conspiracy that exists only in the warped minds of the few. The list of wacky stuff goes on and on. No more fanning the flames of violence through conspiracy theories. It's time for the party to put the kibosh on this. It didn't work in 2020 or in 2022; it won't work in 2024. Tolerate no more nonsense from the Marjorie Taylor Greenes, Lauren Boeberts, Paul Gosars, etc., ad nauseam ad insanis. Argue policy based on those pesky things called facts. Show how your policy decisions are better for the country. Act like adults.

Second, they must stop the juvenile shout-downs during congressional sessions.

That photo of Greene yelling at Joe Biden during the State of the Union address has gone viral, showing Greene in a wild hyena-like pose. While it may sell in some quarters, it's not a good optic nationwide, which is where presidential votes come from. Party leaders should recall the last time a Republican candidate for president topped the popular vote nationwide. Party faithful should take heed and learn an important lesson: looking and acting like a clown won't cut it.

Third, they must stop lying about election rigging, voter fraud and just about anything Donald Trump and the

Trumpites repeatedly scream about in classic pity party blather.

Trump's name-calling and many rants about his victimization are wearing thin. Besides, his silly nicknames for opponents, again while accepted by the way-out-there far right, are more of a reflection on him. People generally want their elected leaders to be the adults in the room. This kind of behavior cuts against that grain. In short, the party needs to grow up and show it can lead. Leadership is not about name-calling or generally acting like a buffoon; it's about policy and ideas that benefit all Americans. Party leaders must show all Americans by words and deeds that they can lead; that they can persuade voters that the party is the better choice. And they must call out threats of violence born of repeated lies. Allowing words of anger and revenge to fester is not leadership; it's culpability.

Fourth, they must show courage and backbone by calling out nonsense when they see and hear it.

When a member of the party says something outlandish or does something stupid, call it out. If a leader cowers in fear of the "party's base" or what a certain candidate for president might do by digging up someone to run against him or her, then that person's spine isn't strong enough to lead. Leadership certainly is not for the wild and woolly; but neither is it for the weak and spineless. Also, party leaders must stop the political stunts like sending migrants to other states, or turning the other cheek when a fraud like

George Santos is among their numbers. Such actions might appeal to the base (which may be dwindling anyway), but it won't expand it...and expanding the base is necessary to win presidential elections.

Fifth, overall, they must stop acting in such a way that being found out becomes a colossal embarrassment.

Through a congressional hearing into the events of January 6, the theft of classified government records, and repeated baseless claims, Trump has now been exposed for what he always was, and what he is. He stands stripped of any honor or dignity he might have had. He is an emperor with no clothes. Sure, he still has millions of loyalists who would support him even if he stood on the Capitol steps and shot someone. But he doesn't have enough votes to win a presidential election; whatever minimal coattails he has won't carry enough candidates to take over the House and Senate....and right now that's all that counts for the party. Learn from the reality of 2020 vs. expectations of a huge red wave. It didn't happen, and it won't happen again unless there is change in how the party offers itself.

As for right wing media, the beating Fox News is taking over knowingly lying on air in support of Trump's lies should send an unmistakable message: if you lie, you will be caught. And once you're caught, you will pay the price that justice exacts. No one knows how much of a financial hit Fox News will take from its lies about Dominion Voting, but it will take a hit. Think rational viewers will look to

Sean Hannity and Tucker Carlson as vicars of truth and wisdom? Fox News generally, and these two pillars of the network, sacrificed themselves on the altar of Trump, and they are paying dearly for it.

There was time when the Republican Party had leaders; Ronald Reagan stands out. So does Dwight Eisenhower and Theodore Roosevelt. Gerald Ford was a decent man. George Bush I held many high offices and was generally respected. Today's leaders need to take lessons from these men, and others who served honorably in Congress and as state leaders who didn't resort to lies, crazy statements, silly stunts, stirring up violence, ignoring blatant embarrassments, acting like children, etc., to make points. It is said people learn more from their failures than their successes. Take heed.

Today's Republican Party must be true to its branding initials GOP: Grand Old Party. Sadly, currently it is not.

IS TRUMP HELPING HIMSELF BY BLASTING DESANTIS?

Hardly a day goes by now that beleaguered former president Donald Trump isn't leveling some vicious bile at Florida Gov. Ron DeSantis. Trump is hoping his attacks will either force DeSantis to leave the field of Republican presidential candidates (it won't), or reduce DeSantis' standing with the party faithful and in the polls (so far, it hasn't).

If Trump's attacks are unsuccessful in moving the needle in his favor at DeSantis' expense (as well as other potential candidates), the question arises what will he do? Added to this mix is the real possibility of one or more criminal indictments. How will Trump react if he's indicted and DeSantis' poll numbers soar among party loyalists, including the remaining MAGA Republicans?

Trump can't stand to lose, or be viewed by the public as a loser. Ironically, his attacks, if ultimately unsuccessful, may well have that effect. In other words, his own conduct may prove to be his undoing, publicly exposing him as the ultimate loser.

For his part, DeSantis doesn't need to respond to Trump's daily juvenile attacks; the public is well aware of Trump's behavior: his lies, his stoking of violence to avoid being cast as a loser, his theft of classified records, his two impeachments, and on and on.

The more Trump attacks DeSantis, the more credibility he gives to his targeted opponent. Each trumped up slogan raises DeSantis' standing as a serious threat to Trump's leadership of the party. It stands to reason that the more publicity Trump gives to DeSantis, the more it focuses the party faithful to view DeSantis as a serious candidate.

So far, DeSantis is playing Trump perfectly. He, as well as many other party leaders, hope Trump will make like a hurricane and eventually blow himself out, sending Trump huffing and puffing into political oblivion. In the meantime, however, DeSantis is saying he's focusing on doing great things to promote freedom in Florida and railing against the evil Biden Administration. This gives pause to the party faithful to place DeSantis' focus on policy alongside Trump's focus on DeSantis, rather than actual governance or leadership.

There is, however, a downside to DeSantis being cast as a frontrunner for the party's presidential nomination. Already, some party leaders are upset at DeSantis' heavy hand in ridding Florida of "wokeness." Trying to cast the definition of "wokeness" as anti-freedom when in reality it means "being alert to and concerned about social injustice and discrimination" or awareness of and sensitivity to social issues, DeSantis' vulnerability is exposed. In this regard, Trump is right when he says DeSantis is trying to re-write history. Whether the messenger in this instance is one who will resonate with the electorate is another matter.

Rather than moderating his stance, since his re-election as governor last year, DeSantis has doubled down on his re-make of Florida government. He exacted vengeance against Disney, threatened to end Advanced Placement classes in Florida, took over a small liberal arts college and vowed to put guardrails on how banks lend money. He has punished political enemies, disrupted institutions, consolidated power and imposed his will on businesses – all in the name of stopping "wokeness."

Unlike Trump, who has no moral compass and no set philosophy of government—except how it can advance his personal brand and image—DeSantis is a true believer.

He's not a phony; he's just dangerous in an authoritarian way.

DeSantis also has the present benefit of a bit of the Teflon effect. Nothing he says or does seems to be diminishing himself in the eyes of potential party voters. Perhaps this is a result, at least in part, of a comparison between him and Trump.

It's safe to say no presidential candidate in our nation's history has the volume of baggage Trump has. A failed presidency; two impeachments; a record of criminal conduct now under investigation in Washington, Georgia and New York (so far as we know; there may be others); and no plan on how he will govern should he return to the White House. His campaign is largely nothing more than a pity party and a barrage against anyone who dares to question, disagree, or run against him.

Also working against him is his age. At a soon-to-be 77, the body and mind can only take so much pent-up rage and anger.

You can bet the mortgage that whatever happens to him as he moves forward toward 2024, he will blame his enemies—real and perceived—for his fate. He will never look in the mirror to find the real source of his many predicaments. His wounds are largely self-inflicted.

Unless DeSantis' numbers begin to drop, either because of Trump's constant barrage, other potential candidates catching fire, or DeSantis' overbearing authoritarian conduct, he will continue to largely sidestep Trump's attacks.

Trump may be compelled to take on such party loyalists like Nikki Haley, Mike Pence, Kristi Noem, Tim Scott, Ted Cruz, Glenn Youngkin, Chris Sununu, Greg Abbott, Larry Hogan, Chris Christie, Asa Hutchinson, Mike Pompeo, Liz Cheney, and John Bolton. Then there are Brian Kemp, Rick Scott and Josh Hawley. Each has visions of sitting behind the famous desk in the Oval Office. To be sure, some will never be taken seriously, others will enjoy having their name floated about for future consideration, or withdraw when moving further appears hopeless.

Trump knows he benefitted from a large field in 2016, but conditions were different then. He was viewed as a successful businessman and TV personality. Now, we know how "successful" he's been, and his media fame no longer masks his ineptitude.

As for the Democrats, Biden will have to deal with the age factor if he chooses to run. But a Trump candidacy also raises the age factor, as the choice would be between and 82-year-old and a 78-year-old. Much has been made by Republicans and some Democrats that Biden doesn't seem all there mentally. Of course, Republicans were silent when Trump's behavior raised the same concerns. Trump's niece, and a few psychologists, even wrote books questioning Trump's mental fitness.

A Biden-Trump repeat would be a wash on the mental fitness issue with one difference: Biden will be running on policy successes and initiatives; Trump will be running on anger and rage. The additional question that Trump will face is how much can his body and mind take of 24-hour pressure like that? He knows if he isn't the nominee, or he loses to Biden again, he will forever be marked as the ultimate loser. That's a lot of self-inflicted pressure on an aged body.

If Biden chooses to pack it in, the Democrats have a host of candidates who would be strong candidates, such as Govs. Gavin Newson, Gretchen Whitmer and J. K. Pritzker. Republicans will predictably rely on their time-worn cliches: liberal, tax and spend, socialist, and on and on ad nauseam. It didn't work against Obama or Biden. Perhaps cooler heads in the party will focus on policy rather than labels and name-calling.

The Democrats can take their time now and see if the Republican Party self-destructs. A Trump-DeSantis war could certainly have that effect, especially if Trump, the sore loser he is, decides to bolt and form a third party, or pull the same kind of stunt that quite possibly cost the party the senate seat in Georgia.

The ball is in the Republican Party's court. Let's see how they play it.

DESANTIS IS NOW AN EXPERT ON
INTERNATIONAL AFFAIRS

As if to prove he has what it takes to be president, Florida Gov. Ron DeSantis chimed in on President Biden's surprise visit to Ukraine, offering his view that perhaps we shouldn't be providing aid to Ukraine in its efforts to deal with Russia's invasion of this sovereign nation.

No, says DeSantis, there is no need to keep giving aid to Ukraine because Russia has proven that it's no longer a first-class military might; Russia isn't really that much of a threat anymore; and in any event the real threat is China. As he said: "I think Russia has been really, really wounded here. And I don't think that they are the same threat to our country, even though they're hostile. I don't think they're on the same level as a China." Whatever the facts may be are unimportant to him; rather, it's what he thinks that matters.

If anyone has any doubt about DeSantis' ambition to run for the presidency, this should dispel it.

Someone needs to tell DeSantis that one of the main reasons Russia has been wounded is the amount of military aid we've been providing to Ukraine since Russia invaded that country a year ago. But these details evidently don't matter to Florida's self-professed leading expert on international affairs.

DeSantis views the current aid level as being a "blank check." I have to believe he knows that whatever aid is offered, it has to be approved by Congress. There is no "blank check" here; while he might sell this line to his supporters, it's absolutely bogus.

DeSantis also used the president's surprise visit to blame Biden for the "disastrous" withdrawal from Afghanistan, the China balloon floating over America, and just about everything else under the sun that he might be able pin on Biden. Never mind his overlooking Biden's predecessor's handling of international events, DeSantis is running for president and he has to show his credentials. Therefore, anything Biden says or does is fair game.

He hasn't finished using his heavy autocratic hand to turn Florida into something resembling the 1920s; now he has to show his global knowledge by waxing on international affairs.

I'm sure Russian strongman Vladimir Putin is shaking in his boots over the prospect of America ending its aid to Ukraine. The leaders of Moldova, Estonia, Latvia, Lithuania, etc., must be clapping their hands in glee over the prospect that, if DeSantis has his way, they will be left to fend for themselves if Putin decides to move forward on rebuilding the Soviet empire one conquest at a time.

If DeSantis is waxing the isolationist line, he had better brush up on his history—the part that he hasn't tried to re-write yet—about the time isolationists ruled Congress less than 100 years ago.

That was in the 1930s, when Hitler was conquering one European country after another. Austria — March 12, 1938; Czechoslovakia — September 29, 1938;

Poland — September 01, 1939; Finland on November 30, 1939; Denmark and Norway — April 09, 1940; France, Belgium, Netherlands, Luxembourg — May 10, 1940; Greece — April 06, 1941; Yugoslavia (modern Albania, Croatia, Montenegro, North Macedonia, and Serbia) — April 06, 1941; The Soviet Union — June 22, 1941; Lithuania, Latvia, and Estonia (Soviet territories) — June 22, 1941; Ukraine — June 22, 1941. The pattern is self-evident.

After British ships were sunk by Germany in early 1940, British Prime Minister Winston Churchill urged President Franklin Roosevelt to provide aid to his beleaguered country, but Roosevelt, cautious of the isolationists in Congress, couldn't respond quickly as he had wanted to; he had to move very carefully before going forward with his Lend-Lease program. Still, America couldn't go any further even as Hitler was invading one country after another because of the strong isolationist mood of the Congress. Leaders of the isolationists, notably Charles Lindbergh, even urged the government to appease Hitler. What a brilliant idea that turned out to be.

It took Pearl Harbor to silence the isolationists and allow our nation to re-tool its infrastructure via an unprecedented mobilization effort, and wage an ultimately successful war against Hitler and the Axis nations, although at the time of the December 7, 1941, attack, our nation wasn't ready for war due largely to the isolationists.

The isolationist movement failed during the 1930s and 1940s, and it will fail again should certain politicians have their way and re-institute it as our nation's international policy.

Despots must know that an attack on a sovereign solely to expand power and influence will be met with a united force led by the world's greatest Democracy. Sending a message that, if elected, these despots won't have to worry about the United States providing aid is precisely the wrong message—and a dangerous one at that.

Dictators know only force; removing that element gives them a free hand; just look at how Hitler accumulated power unchecked during the 1930s. History is a great teacher; but its lessons must be learned or the dire consequences will be repeated.

DeSantis should know whereof he speaks before making comments that might be viewed favorably by our enemies.

SOCIAL SECURITY AND MEDICARE ARE SAFE FOR NOW, BUT ETERNAL VIGILANCE IS NECESSARY

When Florida Sen. Rick Scott proposed "sunsetting" all programs after five years, including Social Security and Medicare, he hit such a raw nerve that not only Democrats, but many Republicans called him out.

Sunsetting is a legislative process that allows programs to automatically terminate after a period of years, subjecting any re-enactment to passage just as any other bill. Scott well knows that passing a bill is much harder than repealing one; thus, any effort to re-enact Social Security or Medicare would require a majority vote of both houses of Congress, and the president's signature. To see how hard it is to pass a bill, check out efforts to adopt a national law on abortion or a ban on assault rifles and adoption of common sense gun regulations, such as universal background checks.

Scott is not some ordinary back-seat member of the Senate; he is the chairman of the National Republican Senatorial Committee, so when he says something, even if outrageous, he's listened to. As a hard-right conservative, Scott has long advocated "sunsetting" all federal programs every five years. What certainty this gives to such bedrock programs as Social Security, the nation's safety net for retirees and others, and Medicare, apparently gives Scott no pause.

Nevertheless, after being roundly criticized by leaders of both parties, Scott finally backed down, saying that "Social Security, Medicare, national security, veterans' benefits and other essential services" should not have to re-justify their existence.

For the time being, therefore, Social Security and Medicare, as well as other programs in Scott's line of sight, are safe. But there's no guarantee this won't change down the road.

Scott's plan certainly is a non-starter now, but if the Republicans gain control of both houses of Congress and the White House, I'm not so sure Social Security as we know it will survive. There are studies that show some sustainability problems in the next decade, but they can be addressed by changing eligibility requirements and level of payment to those making big bucks in retirement anyway. The same can be said for Medicare.

My concern is once they get their hands on the entire social network system, how far might they go to revamp it, watering it down to such an extent that its historic function as a true safety net is vitiated.

Currently, Florida looks like a petri dish for what could happen at the federal level. If Florida Gov. Ron DeSantis becomes president and is given the kind of Congress he has with the Florida legislature—a strong Republican majority--who's to say what brakes would be applied to their efforts at targeting Social Security, Medicare and other similar type programs?

As far as resorting to the courts, running to the courts in Florida is not so great a fear for the Republicans; DeSantis has succeeded in large part in re-shaping the state judiciary to fit his purposes. As president, DeSantis would have the opportunity to appoint like-minded lawyers to the federal judiciary. And if not DeSantis, another one like him would be just as much a threat to these programs. The current version of the former GOP wants to roll back many of the progressive programs brought about by historic economic and social conditions; what is to prevent them from adding Social Security and Medicare to the mix?

It can't be emphasized enough that it's much harder to kill an existing program than to enact one. Further, majority rule doesn't sway the Republicans. If it did, abortion would still be permitted under the Constitution or a law would be enacted protecting a woman's right to an abortion, and there would be a ban on assault weapons and a system of universal background checks. Even though a majority of Americans favor these proposals, try getting any of them through Congress today.

Scott revealed his true feelings when he talked of the kind of knife he wanted to take to Social Security and Medicare. Any tinkering in the name of reform exposes these programs to Scott's stated personal goal. In the name of reform, he and his backers could do real damage to them.

Right now in Florida, Republicans are busy "reforming" education by banning books, re-writing history and cleansing curriculum; "reforming" the relationship between business and government by allowing punitive suits against government regulations the right wing doesn't like; "reforming" state and local government relations by dictating to local governments what they can and cannot regulate; all after "reforming" state election laws by restricting access to voting. They are doing all of this in the name of freedom.

If they get to take this "freedom" juggernaut to Washington, who knows the amount of damage they could do to our Democratic form of government. Taking our nation back to the days of unregulated business of the 1920s or the isolationism of the 1930s resulted in dire consequences economically—the Great Depression--and internationally—World War II--that almost destroyed our country. We can't afford to have the current iteration of the Republican Party take us back in time.

Yes, the threat to Social Security and Medicare has diminished for the time being. But to assure no further threat to these and other social programs exists down the road, it will take eternal vigilance by all citizens who benefit—or will benefit in the future—from these programs.

WHAT ARE REPUBLICANS DRINKING?

A Republican Wisconsin judge who helped Donald Trump in his failed effort to overturn the 2020 election advanced toward a seat on the state's Supreme Court. I suppose for those Wisconsin voters, helping a losing president advance a lie in the courts is the kind of justice they want on the state's highest court.

Not to be outdone in the Department of Outrageousness, Rep. Marjorie Taylor Greene of Georgia, who is <u>well known for speaking her mind before putting her brain in gear,</u> resurrected her call for a "national divorce," arguing that Republican and Democratic states needed to be separated. Never mind the Constitution and laws of our nation; never mind our nation's history; and never mind the words of the oath of office she took, rather than reconsidering the absurdity of her comment, she doubled down when called out by those of sane mind.

Rather than backing down, which she doesn't do regardless of the craziness of her blather, she added yet another asinine statement to her growing list by saying Democrats who move to Republican-run states shouldn't be allowed to vote for five years. Again, the federal Constitution, laws of the land, the nation's history and her oath of office obviously don't operate as a check on her craziness.

For all of her wackiness, House Speaker Kevin McCarthy continues to support her, saying he will always have her back. It's not her back that's so ridiculous; it's the drivel that pours forth from her mouth. One would think the competent members of the Republican Party would be embarrassed by such behavior from a member of Congress. Except for an occasional jibe from Mitt Romney, the party leadership isn't willing to put the kibosh on this lunacy. Meanwhile, pathological liar George Santos still sits in the House of Representatives as if nothing untoward has happened.

And then there are those who, despite all of the demonstrated wacky and criminal behavior of Donald Trump, think Joe Biden is far a worse president than the MAGA guru. Never mind that not a single respected historian agrees with this unsupported assessment; never mind that these Trump diehards can't point to a single policy initiative that supposedly made America great again (except for a tax cut largely for the wealthy and packing the Supreme Court with right wing ideologues), they simply choose to believe what they want to believe. For them, facts don't matter.

I don't recall Biden seeking election help in 2020 by holding back federal funds from a foreign nation in return for dirt on his opponent. I don't recall Biden fomenting an attack on the nation's capital to promote his lie about a rigged election. I don't recall Biden deliberately stealing classified records from the White House, strewing them around his estate, and then ridiculously claiming he declassified them "just by thinking about it." These are the actions of a narcissistic, egomaniacal authoritarian, but in the eyes of those who choose not to see, he was a better president than Biden. Trump faces the profound prospects of criminal prosecution on many fronts; yet, somehow, there are still those who rigidly cling to the bogus notion that Trump is a great man and was a great president.

To be sure, everyone is entitled to his or her own opinion. However, it's helpful when opinion is supported by fact rather than pure belief. Of course, Biden has his faults; in fact, all presidents had their faults. That's part of the human experience. But to favorably compare Trump with Biden on facts alone is laughable. Next thing you know, they'll opine that Trump is smarter, kinder, more compassionate and has a bigger heart than Jimmy Carter.

What is so disconcerting is that even after all the things we've learned about Trump over the past several years; even after Republican candidates and officeholders continued to spread election lies; and even after what we've learned about a certain right wing media outlet that continued to knowingly spread an election fraud lie to its viewing audience; they still enjoy the support of millions of Republicans.

The Republican Party has to have a better candidate pool to choose from; candidates that are competent, intelligent and articulate. If the party showed courage and integrity, it would have no legitimate reason to give favor to a fraud-pushing judge in Wisconsin; a weird loudmouth congresswoman from Georgia; and a seriously flawed and failed ex-president, among others.

To the voters in Wisconsin who want a fraud pusher on their top court; to the millions who still support Trump—crimes, warts and all; to those who still support the liars, election deniers and conspiracy theorists, there is this one question:

What are Republicans drinking?

"A BASKET OF DEPLORABLES"

During a speech in 2016, Hillary Clinton made a comment that would dog her throughout her campaign for the presidency against Donald Trump. She said half of Trump's supporters belong in a "basket of deplorables" characterized by "racist, sexist, homophobic, xenophobic, Islamaphobic" views. "Unfortunately there are people like that. And (Trump) has lifted them up."

In so many words, Clinton said millions of Americans deserved to be strongly condemned, censured or held in contempt for their un-American views. This was strong stuff back then, and she was roundly vilified for her remarks.

But if she made that same accusation today, would she be wrong? And if other types of behavior were included, would "deplorable" be a proper description? Let's see.

Attacks on Black churches and Jewish synagogues by white supremacists and neo-Nazis. Is this deplorable?

Neo-Nazis march on public streets screaming anti-Semitic slurs and denying the Holocaust. Is this deplorable?

Elected officials remain silent in the face of these attacks by white supremacists and neo-Nazis. Is this deplorable?

Lying about election results and fomenting violence in the name of that lie. Is this deplorable?

Public officials provide aid and comfort to that liar by supporting him even while knowing of the lie. Is this deplorable?

A senator pumps his fist in support of rioters' attack on the government. Is this deplorable?

A member of Congress who hopes to be vice president someday advocates a "national divorce" between red and blue states, and proffers that Democrats who move into GOP-run states shouldn't be allowed to vote for five years. Is this deplorable?

A member of Congress screams "liar" at the top of her lungs while the president is delivering the important State of the Union address to Congress and the nation. Is this deplorable?

A sitting president asks a foreign head of state for campaign dirt on his opponent in return for release of congressionally approved funds. Is this deplorable?

A sitting president leaves office, absconding with classified records that are supposed to go to the National Archives. He takes them to his home, strews them about where they can be read by anyone, and claims he can declassify them by simply "thinking about it." Is this deplorable?

A national news network repeats lie after lie to its viewers, all while the top brass and its TV stars knew the truth. Is this deplorable?

In defense of these lies, the network maintains the First Amendment allows for the broadcast of knowing lies, even if the subject of those lies suffers financial losses. Is this deplorable?

The party that once stood staunchly for law-and-order reverses course after an FBI raid that uncovers stolen government records, stirring up opposition to the FBI and tapping into political grievances and far-right conspiracies rather than the crime itself. Is this deplorable?

A governor says that a white nationalist candidate is better than a Democrat. Is this deplorable?

After each mass shooting, public officials wax "thoughts and prayers," yet fail to take action to prevent these random crimes. Is this deplorable?

These are examples that come immediately to mind; I could go on and on, listing conduct similar in gravity and hubris to these over the past several years. I could also add government behavior in the several states, most notably Florida as its governor ratchets up his campaign for president--such as attacking academic freedom, politicizing school boards and education generally, mandating far-right conservative indoctrination, punishing those who refuse to bend to his command, etc., all in the name of freedom, but the point is made.

Has what was once spoken in the darkest of corners and remotest of caves now made acceptable public discourse and behavior by our elected officials, and their diehard supporters? And is this in itself deplorable?

Was Hillary Clinton flat-out wrong in 2016, or was she looking into a crystal ball, accurately predicting the future for our country?

To be sure, there are those who believe that when it comes to the Clintons, there seems to be some black kettles being thrown at glass houses, believing she is herself a deplorable--especially her husband. I don't doubt or excuse some of their fast and loose behavior.

The sad fact is the Clintons are not alone; other top elected officials throughout history have operated in the shadows in varying degrees. Teapot Dome, Watergate, Iran-Contra, it's all there. But for me, there is no comparison to what I've listed to what the Clintons are reputed to have done. What the Clintons did largely profited themselves. Clinton's impeachment was over his personal moral behavior. What the Clintons did was not an effort to undermine our fundamental form of government. Can't say the same about what I've listed above.

Some believe that one day the truth is going to come out about the Clintons, averring that their conduct goes far deeper than what most liberal Democrats would have us think. This may be true, but our system of justice requires proof beyond a reasonable doubt; speculation and belief will not convict, and neither will gut feelings.

There is another scenario that must be borne in mind. For purely investigative purposes, from 2013 to 2021, Republicans held at least one house of Congress; from 2015 to 2019, the party controlled both houses, and for two of those years, the party had Trump in the White House. Republicans had ample time to make their case, including years when the party had both houses of Congress, the White House, the Justice Department, etc., and so far, Republicans produced nothing against either one. Every lawyer knows that time is an enemy; people grow old, memories fade, they die off. The time to strike in any criminal case is as close to the events as possible. Hillary Clinton hasn't held office since 2013; Bill Clinton was out of office in 2003. If there's a criminal case to be made against either or both, those who want this had better hurry up. They had their chance against Bill with Whitewater, and against Hillary with Benghazi and email.

Right now, House Republicans are focused on Hunter Biden, Joe Biden and everything else Biden. If they truly believe they had a chance to make a case against the Clintons, they would be salivating at the bit to move forward. But they're not, probably because they privately agree with what then-FBI Director Jim Comey concluded--that there simply was no criminal case that could be made against Hillary for misuse of her email account. I think it's safe to say there is a far greater likelihood that one or more criminal charges will be filed against Trump and one or more of his cohorts than against either Clinton.

Finally, what can be said about the tens of millions who still believe, despite overwhelming evidence to the contrary, that Trump did no wrong; that the election was stolen from him; that what happened on January 6 was just a few supporters engaging in legitimate political discourse, that Trump never lied, etc., etc., etc.? Are these people considered deplorables?

WHAT WILL POLITICAL LEADERSHIP LOOK LIKE TEN YEARS FROM NOW?

Considering our nation's deep divide between red states and blue states, liberals and conservatives; with moderates seemingly becoming a dying breed, it's fair to ask what our federal government will look like down the road; say, ten years from now.

What image will fit the presidential mold voters will be looking for? Will it be a Jimmy Carter or Ronald Reagan? Bill Clinton or George Bush (choose whichever)? Barack Obama or Donald Trump? Perhaps a Dwight Eisenhower or a Harry Truman? Maybe a Franklin Roosevelt or a Richard

Nixon? A corollary question is what kind of people will the voters choose that fits their preferred mold?

Maybe none of the above. Maybe we'll continue to search for presidential leadership by choosing one brand, rejecting it, then choosing another, repeating this cycle over and over again, expecting a different result. Come to think of it, that's the definition of insanity.

Just look at the shifts over the past 100 years. Americans had presidents Harding, Coolidge and Hoover; however, they grew tired and angry over the 12-year economic mess they gave us, so Americans shifted to Roosevelt and Truman. But they grew tired of them and their liberal policies and shifted to moderate Dwight Eisenhower. But in 1960, voters grew tired of "old man" Ike and didn't want "Tricky" Richard Nixon, so they went with a young and vigorous John Kennedy. But after his successor, Lyndon Johnson, angered the south with his civil rights stand and angered voters generally with his prosecution of the Vietnam War, voters grew weary and resorted to the old stand-by who branded himself as the "New" Richard Nixon who successfully tapped into the law and order theme. However, with the Watergate scandal Nixon proved to be the same "Tricky Dick" they rejected in 1960, and Gerald Ford's pardon of Nixon, the voters were angry enough that they chose a new face, Jimmy Carter, who promised never to lie to them.

But Carter proved too much of a technician and too little of a crisis manager who famously said a malaise was gripping the nation, so the electorate chose the handsome and theatrical Ronald Reagan. But after Iran-Contra and George Bush I's feckless handling of the economy, the voters chose the young, brash but centrist Bill Clinton. But after his peccadillos, yet again the voters tired and turned to George Bush II. Then came Iraq and a few other missteps, and voters made a drastic turn toward Barack Obama. But lots of folks rebelled against a Black man in the Oval Office, and a firebrand TV personality and putative successful businessman Donald Trump tapped into anger, resentment and downright hatred simmering below the surface and gave it life. And that package, along with the missteps of Hillary Clinton and her mishandling of her government email account so soon after Benghazi, propelled Trump to the White House.

Trump's four years of misstep after misstep proving this emperor had no clothes, however, led to enough embarrassments that voters tossed him out of office after one term—joining Hoover, Carter and Bush I as one-term presidents over the last century. (Coolidge, Johnson and Ford don't count because they served part of another's term.)

Now, it's Joe Biden, 80 years old and angling to be re-elected which, if successful, will make him 86 when he leaves after two full terms. Considering the average life expectancy is around 78, re-electing him might be a dicey prospect.

And then there's Donald Trump, who at 78 also must face the age issue. If he should pull a Grover Cleveland and serve non-consecutive terms, he will be 82 when he leaves office. (This of course assumes quite a bit, but there's no harm in speculating.)

The Republican Party has enough folks who dream of living in the White House and, should Trump fall or be pushed over the cliff, would gladly jump at the chance to state their claim to the presidency. Party faithful who are salivating at the chance to take their case to the public include such luminaries as Ron DeSantis, Mike Pence, Greg Abbott, Mike Pompeo, Josh Hawley, and Ted Cruz. These are just a few who come immediately to mind. There will undoubtedly be others should lightning strike causing images of greatness to dance in their heads.

For the Democrats, there is Vice President Kamala Harris, Govs. Gavin Newsom, Gretchen Whitmer, J. K. Pritzker, and who knows who else might rise to the top of the party's list over the next few years depending on unforeseen circumstances.

With regard to both parties, it's entirely possible other candidates may emerge who aren't in the public's line of sight yet.

GEORGE WAAS

By the end of this decade, both Biden and Trump will be gone, and both parties will need to assess where they want to take the country as our nation moves from its 250th anniversary in 2026 to its 300th birthday in 2076. There's a lot of water that will flow under the nation's bridge between now and then, but if there is one thing that is certain, each party will pitch its age-old philosophy hoping voters will buy it as the guiding force for the future.

Historically, voters generally believed they were trending toward effective leaders; leaders who could provide both a vision and plan for America. It's easy to point out the general principles of effective leadership: honesty, compassion, intelligence, competence, wisdom, belief in purpose, taking full responsibility, the ability to move on and forgive, humility, optimism mixed with realism, valuing others' opinions while having confidence in your own., and on and on.

But after the last few years, these bedrock principles have taken a hit borne of the politics of anger, resentment, and rage. Lies have become acceptable. Lashing out at enemies more imagined than real has become fashionable. Criminal conduct has been largely overlooked under the rubric of "whataboutism," or deflected by creating scapegoats. The politics of reason and compromise best characterized by Ronald Reagan and Tip O'Neill have been replaced by the politics of hatred and violence.

The question thus becomes what are American voters looking for? Do they really know what they want from their government? Do they want policies that make their lives better, or are they satisfied with rage that allows them to vent their spleen at their "enemies?"

There is no doubt each political party will press its usual standard line: from the Republicans, it will continue to be limited government, less taxes, free enterprise, law and order, personal accountability. (Whether the party leaders practice what they preach or explain what they really mean by these soundbites is another matter.)

For the Democrats, it's about promoting social programs and supporting labor unions, consumer protection, workplace safety regulation, equal opportunity, disability rights, racial equity, regulations against environmental pollution, and criminal justice reform. (Of course, the devil's in the details.)

In 2008 and 2012, voters elected liberal Black Barack Obama as president. Four years later, voters elected hard-right authoritarian and rage engine Donald Trump. This 180-degree dichotomy between these two presidents and their approach toward government make me wonder whether the voters really know what they want. Perhaps it's just a matter of not liking the status quo or the incumbent. Perhaps it's a matter of which party can best sell their bill of goods. Maybe the voters really don't know what they want, but they're not satisfied with what they have.

This recalls the old saw that the intelligence of the voting public shouldn't be underestimated. Of course, the cynical corollary to this is the intelligence of the voting public shouldn't be overrated, either.

Considering the volatility of the American voter, I doubt we will see more than an eight-year run of one-party control of the White House; the same may be said for both houses of Congress. No more three consecutive GOP terms like we had with Reagan and Bush I. No more runs of eight years or more for a House speaker or Senate majority leader. I think our nation is in the age of political see-sawing between the major parties.

Regardless of what the respective political parties pitch to the voters down the road, their talking points will take a back seat to the larger and more profound question: what will the voters accept as true that will make them go to the polls?

The future of our country hangs on the answer to that question.

KEVIN MCCARTHY HAS SOLD HIS SOUL TO THE EXTREME RIGHT WING OF HIS PARTY. HERE'S A CLEAR EXAMPLE

House Speaker Kevin McCarthy could have turned over his videos of the January 6 riot at the capital to a legitimate investigatory body, such as the House committee charged with investigating that insurrection. He could have turned them over to the Department of Justice. He could have even turned them over to a legitimate news network.

He did neither. Instead, fulfilling a promise to the extreme right of his party in return for the speakership, he gave those videos to Fox News. You will recall Fox and its two media stars, Sean Hannity and Tucker Carlson, were recently outed for pushing Donald Trump's rigged election Big Lie, targeting the voting machines owned by Dominion Voting Systems, even as they knew they were repeatedly broadcasting a lie to their audience.

For its defense, Fox News maintains the First Amendment protects their statements because of their newsworthiness and that these statements constitute core political speech for which the First Amendment accords the highest protection from liability.

What is newsworthy about a deliberate, known lie is not the election itself; it's the lie. Fox made the lie a newsworthy event; that's why this is being reported by all legitimate news sources, but not by Fox because it no longer has any claim of reportorial legitimacy. Reporting on an election is core political speech; deliberately lying about is not protected by the First Amendment.

Dominican has sued Fox and its stars for defamation. The current legal standard for proving defamation committed by public figures such as Hannity and Carlson requires Dominion to show that Fox and its mouthpieces acted with actual malice. In other words, that they knew that the statement was false—or they acted with reckless disregard for whether the statement was true or false.

Dominion has them on both counts. First, the evidence presented to the court handling its defamation case has the "smoking gun" testimony from the network's executives and hosts privately blasting the election fraud claims being peddled by Trump's team, yet allowing lies about the 2020 contest to be repeatedly promoted on the air to its fawning audience in an effort to boost ratings. To put it directly, they knew Trump's claim of a rigged election was false yet persisted in passing along the Big Lie to their uncritical viewers in part by baselessly attacking Dominion for being part of a non-existent conspiracy.

Dominion doesn't even have to get to the second prong because there is no greater reckless disregard than knowing the truth without reservation, yet intentionally lying about it on the air.

McCarthy certainly sold his soul to the extremists in his party. Sadly, he won't be held accountable because the House is in his party's hands. In his pitiful defense, he said he "promised" fellow well-known flamethrower Matt Gaetz he'd turn over the videos; he just didn't say to whom.

Judging from previous conduct, we can expect Fox and Carlson to slice, dice, splice, etc., those tapes and present their false version of what transpired on January 6. They will do anything and everything to try to justify the lies they began spinning on that fateful day when some government officials tossed their oaths of office into the trash, and Fox News tossed the journalism code of ethics into the fire.

Ironically, this comes at a time when the right wing wants to tamp down the standard for proving a defamation case. Trump and a few of his cohorts, past and present, want to make it easier to sue CNN, MSNBC, CBS, ABC, etc. To show how little they've thought this through, whatever they can get the Supreme Court to do to make it easier to sue news networks will also make it easier to sue Fox and other networks who choose to peddle lies and propaganda over hard news.

While Fox is on the hot seat for millions of dollars in damages, the executives and media stars need not worry about their audience. The millions who salivate over the Hannitys and Carlsons will continue to blindly follow their pied pipers, gleefully ingesting the garbage they are being fed, and clapping and doing a happy dance over their self-serving belief that they are being well informed.

"SHAMELESS"

A few years ago, Showtime aired a series called "Shameless." It was offered as an American comedy drama that ran from 2011 to 2021.

The series depicted the poor, dysfunctional family of Frank Gallagher, a neglectful single father of six who spent his days drunk, high, or in search of misadventures, while his children learned to take care of themselves, occasionally engaging in their own misadventures. For all his transgressions, Gallagher never showed any shame or remorse. He couldn't show any second-thought emotion because he had no sense of compassion. He was, as the show's title says, shameless.

"Shameless" means "insensible to disgrace; showing a lack of shame." It can also mean a lack of a sense of conscience that allows for the showing of remorse for deviant behavior. What is essential is that the subject be aware of bad behavior.

Against this backdrop, shameless is a most appropriate description of today's version of the Republican Party. Putting it bluntly, far too many of the party's leaders and spokespersons have no shame, no conscience and no awareness of bad behavior.

Words you will never hear uttered by these extremists include: "I'm sorry." "I made a mistake." "I was wrong." "I apologize." "It won't happen again." "I ask for your forgiveness and understanding."

Rather than admitting to human frailties and showing compassion and a sense of conscience, they will double down on their aberrant ways, saying in effect: "Yeah, so what?" "What are you going to do about it?" "Too bad; that's tough," and other similar brush-offs of their critics, demonstrating their disdain for the general public (but not for the loyal masses who gobble up what they dish out.)

Some examples make the point.

Donald Trump's incompetent rollout of the government's initial response to the COVID pandemic undoubtedly cost lives. No apology.

Shameless.

He illegally called the Ukraine president seeking dirt on Hunter Biden in exchange for release of congressionally appropriated funds. For this "high crime and misdemeanor," he offered no apology; rather, he doubled down, calling the call "perfect."

Shameless.

He fanned the flames of a riotous crowd of loyalists on January 6 to support his rigged election lie, telling them to go to the capital and save the country. Five died that day because of his "high crimes and misdemeanors" and criminal acts; several law enforcement officers committed suicide. Yet, he never apologized for his damnable actions.

Shameless.

He intentionally stole confidential government records, and even after the government made requests for their return, still kept them at his estate, spreading them around like yesterday's newspaper. Rather than fessing up to his behavior, he said he could classify them by thinking about it. Of course, he offered no apology.

Shameless.

Dozens of members of Congress backed Trump's election lie—some to this day remain election deniers with no facts to support their nonsensical belief. Yet, no apology; no admission of a mistake or the recognition that they had no basis for their action.

Shameless.

House Speaker Kevin McCarthy turned over his videos of January 6 not to a legitimate investigative body, but to a news network that has been outed as a liar that deliberately damaged a voting equipment company to appease Trump and improve its ratings. No request for forgiveness. No admission of any wrongdoing. Instead, the network, Fox News, is relying on a ludicrous interpretation of the First Amendment that a first-year law student would be embarrassed to make.

Shameless.

McCarthy and his Judiciary Committee Chairman Jim Jordan, both under the House Ethics Committee jurisdiction for their culpability in the January 6 insurrection, are not investigating Trump, their own conduct, or the others in their party who tried to undermine the Constitutionally mandated certification of the 2020 election. Rather, they are investigating Hunter Biden, who's been under investigation since before Joe Biden began his term more than two years ago. By avoiding an obvious investigation in favor of a scapegoated one, they should show some self-doubt. Sadly, there is none.

Shameless.

Sen. Josh Hawley fist-pumped support for the January 6 rioters.

Shameless.

The Republican National Committee declared that the insurrection was nothing more than a few loyal supporters engaging in legitimate political discourse.

Shameless.

Marjorie Taylor Greene, Lauren Boebert and others in Congress and the media continue to engage in juvenile, embarrassing behavior, with no accountability.

Shameless.

George Santos lied his way to Congress, yet there is no accountability for his disgraceful behavior.

Shameless.

Not to be outdone, Shamelessness applies to some state elected leaders, most notably Florida Gov. Ron DeSantis, who can't seem to do enough to please the extremists in his party.

After undermining academic freedom by restricting what can be taught in schools; after banning books he finds objectionable; after putting his thumb on local governments; after foregoing safety for open carry of guns without a permit; and after attacking officeholders who dare to disagree with him by expressing their personal views (of course, DeSantis expresses his personal views every chance he gets); he has now decided to take on advanced placement classes in the high schools.

Shameless.

Advanced Placement is a program run by the College Board (the makers of the SAT) that allows students to take special high school courses that can earn them college credit and/ or qualify them for more advanced classes when they begin college.

AP classes are designed to give students the experience of an entry-level college class while still in high school, earning college credit for the class if they pass the AP exam.

These classes are for "the best and the brightest;" the students who will improve Florida's rank among the best education systems in America.

But DeSantis and his minions can't have that. They can't have intelligent, well-educated students who are smart enough to question authority and understand when they are being conned. Whatever these right wing leaders say must be accepted as gospel. These faux leaders know best, and who are these students—these so-called "best and the brightest"--to dare to challenge them? Such unmitigated audacity to have students think for themselves!

Their message is these students must not become independent thinkers; they must do as they are told. These false prophets can't have students (and when they grow up and become adults) asking difficult questions they can't answer, or that the answers will prove embarrassing. There must be no critical thinking and no rational explanations. They will tell students what to read; what to study; what to think; what to say and what to write. And they will tell them this is what real freedom is about! And the dumbed-down mind will accept this without question!

Shameless.

Rather than trying to raise Florida's educational standards higher, DeSantis and his kind are hard at work turning Florida's education system into a Mississippi, Louisiana or West Virginia.

By way of example, Mississippi's school system ranks 48th for spending. The state ranks 42nd for highest percentage of injured/threatened high school students and is tied with Louisiana, South Carolina, Hawaii and Nevada at 47th for lowest median ACT score. Mississippi ranks 45th in safety and 43rd in quality. This is what DeSantis and his lemmings want for Florida. They don't want to lift us up; they want to dumb us down.

Shameless.

These people must make certain that Florida doesn't improve its education standards among the several states; rather, it's more important for them to assure that every person is armed even if not trained and have no permit. For them, it's more important for people to proudly display their firearms in malls, schools, shopping centers, parking lots, etc., than it is to have "the best and the brightest" minds among us.

Shameless.

To top this off, Gov. Ron DeSantis and his legislative cohorts have introduced a most draconian and dangerous piece of legislation designed to undermine the very foundation of our education system. It's contained in HB 999. Make no mistake about it, this bill, if passed, is a frontal assault on education.

Quoting one part of what this bill covers makes my point. The bill requires general education courses to "promote the values necessary to preserve the constitutional republic through traditional, historically accurate, and high-quality coursework," and cannot be "based on unproven, theoretical, or exploratory content."

Focus on the prohibition against teaching anything that is "theoretical." There are educational courses that are based on theory. Science embraces many courses based on theory, like the Theory of Relativity. Are these courses to be axed?

What about religion classes? Religion is based, at least in part, on theories, or unproven beliefs. Indeed, belief lies at the heart of religion. Are these courses to be axed as well? A cursory check on Google of theories that are taught as part of an education system reveals a rather lengthy list. Are these to be abolished as part of this curriculum cleansing program?

Cooler, calmer, saner heads must go through this legislation with a fine tooth comb and address the real harm this will cause if this bill becomes law. Critics who have analyzed this bill ask the question: what will be allowed to be taught that will encourage the critical inquiring mind, instead of blindly accepting what is dished out in the name of knowledge?

Shameless.

ANOTHER COMMENT ABOUT A PROPOSED LAW THAT IS DESTRUCTIVE OF FLORIDA EDUCATION

The other day, I commented on HB 599 currently before the Florida Legislature. It's being pushed by Florida Gov. Ron DeSantis and his legislative cronies, so it's highly likely to pass, at least in one form or another. This bill is a sop to the extreme right wing of the Republican Party.

Briefly noted, it would require that general education courses at state colleges and universities "promote the values necessary to preserve the constitutional republic" and cannot define American history "as contrary to the creation of a new nation based on universal principles stated in the Declaration of Independence." It would prohibit general courses "with a curriculum based on unproven, theoretical or exploratory content.

The last sentence means classes couldn't be offered if they dealt with either proving or disproving theories. Presumably, everything taught would have to based on fact. This would seemingly include every subject, including religion. Presumably, there would no longer be any study that sought to test a hypothesis for its veracity. How will they decide exactly what is and isn't theory? And how will current theories ever be proven to be fact or fiction? This says volumes about the value of the inquiring mind, but that's for another day.

Just as vital is the part dealing with the Declaration of Independence. Bear in mind this declaration was a unanimous point-by-point indictment of the tyrannical, authoritarian rule of King George III of England over the 13 colonies/states that made up America. These delegates were throwing off the chains King George shackled around our young nation's citizens. How ironical it is that what Ron DeSantis and his cronies are doing is creating a tyrannical, authoritarian, heavy-handed rule of their own.

The "universal principles" referred to are those "self-evident" truths "that all men are created equal, that they are endowed by their Creator with certain unalienable Rights, that among these are Life, Liberty and the pursuit of Happiness." Note there is no mention of women, and that while "all men are created equal" and "endowed" with "certain unalienable Rights," history tells us this didn't apply to differential treatment based on status or condition. Recall the 3/5th clause dealing with slaves in the original Constitution.

The fact that DeSantis and his Republican acolytes want this bill means it will most assuredly pass, at least in some form. If it does pass, what effect will this language have on the teaching of history? How will such subjects as the Civil War and World War II and the roundup of Japanese-Americans be taught without a discussion of race and ethnicity? How about the historical intersection between race, gender and class? What about teaching law; specifically Supreme Court decisions on race, sex and gender?

In sum, to avoid the type of punishment provided by this legislation for its violations, how will administrators and college instructors match the teachings against the words of the Declaration of Independence?

Some ideological bureaucrats sitting in an office away from colleges and universities will be tasked with making these monumental decisions that will affect the future of our state.

That should send chills up and down the spines of those who value a free and independent system of education designed to create generations of critical thinkers with inquiring minds.

Progress is made by those who ask "Why?" and not those who say "OK, whatever you say."

"TRUE COLORS"

Hardly a day goes by that we don't learn about a person who we thought was the pillar of the community, a person of integrity, only to be revealed as a fraud.

It's this moment of realization that a person shows his true colors.

Showing true colors means showing what a person is really like. It's the moment that person reveals his or her true nature or character. An oft-heard comment may be: "He seemed nice at first, but he showed his true colors during the crisis." How many women have said "I thought he was a really sweet guy, but then he got mad and showed his true colors."

True colors reveals the kind of person someone really is, rather than what the person seems to be. It is the disclosure of one's real character and intentions, especially when these are disreputable or dishonorable.

A classic example in the workforce is: "She was only too anxious to get out of the room now that her employer had shown his true colors."

This phrase dates back to the 1700s. It has a nautical origin and refers to the color of the flag which every ship is required to fly at sea. Pirates used to deceive other ships by sailing under false flags so that they would not excite suspicion. The other ships, thinking that the pirates were friendly, sailed close to them and fell under their grip. It was only after the attack that the pirates would show their 'true flag'.

If someone shows his true colors, he reveals himself as he really is, with no filter. He is laid bare psychologically and emotionally. He is an emperor with no clothes. He acts according to his real personality as opposed to how he's been portrayed or after having been deceptively and deliberately misleading.

Here are a few quotes that exemplify when true colors are revealed. See if they fit into your experiences. I have to believe they do in one form or another.

"She always thought he was completely honest, but he showed his true colors when he cheated on her.

False friends show their true colors when you badly need their help.

John pretended that the deal was in my best interest, but he showed his true colors when I realized that he got a big commission for getting me into an unprofitable sale.

I've known Sandra since we were high school classmates - she's such a mean person. I am sure Alan will eventually discover her true personality. One day, she will show her true colors.

Everybody thought Bob was a cool guy. It was only when he was promoted as a chief manager that he showed his true colors."

You're familiar with the expression: "He's not what he seemed." This is a most appropriate reference to true colors.

Examples abound showing people who were once highly regarded, only to ultimately reveal themselves in a darkly negative light; a con artist, a fraud and worse.

Currently under way is the murder trial Alex Murdaugh, accused of killing his wife and son to deflect from his drug problem and financial mischief. It is such a sensational trial that some TV media have been covering it each day.

The Murdaughs were prominent American legal family in the Low Country region of South Carolina. From 1920 to 2006, three members of the family consecutively served as solicitor (district attorney), in charge of prosecuting all criminal cases in the state's 14th circuit district, leading locals to call the five-county district, "Murdaugh Country."

The family also founded a nationally recognized litigation law firm.

But the Murdaughs have shown their true colors over the past few years through a series of skullduggery, and now Alex Murdaugh has joined other family members in revealing his true colors to the American audience.

Kanye West is a prominent rap artist, winner of many awards. But he revealed his true colors with his anti-Semitic diatribes.

Richard Nixon. Bill Cosby. Harvey Weinstein. R. Kelly. I could go on and on and on with a list that would run many pages mentioning names and their ultimate true color transgressions.

There's another expression that says a person can spend 40 years building a sterling reputation, only to trash it in a few moments. That's another way of revealing true colors.

Donald Trump was reputed to be a successful businessman and host of a popular TV reality show where he famously "fired" people. This only added to his image as tough negotiator and consummate entrepreneur. However, he revealed his true colors during his term as president and in his post-presidency as a cheat, liar, bigot, crook and thief.

There is no doubt you can name entertainers, politicians, lawyers, judges, corporate executives, professionals—the pillars of your community—who ultimately spent time in jail, lost their life savings, and ended up in disgrace as a result of their display of true colors.

Each of you have—and will---come into contact with people who appear kind, gentle, compassionate, intelligent, caring; in short, possessive of all the qualities of a decent human being. But when the chips are down; when the circumstances reach the level that is consequential, crucial, critical, decisive, eventful or far-reaching, that's when they will reveal their true selves—their true colors.

I have little doubt you see people revealing their true colors just about every day. Look in the newspaper, watch TV. You will see people you once thought were the cream of the crop; now, they stand exposed for what they really are by their true colors.

What is essential is that you recognize that falseness at the earliest possible moment. This will at least minimize the extent of the harm or injury caused by putting one's faith in a fraud.

Putting it succinctly, don't allow yourself to be conned. Use good judgment and common sense.

SACRIFICING WISDOM FOR GRATIFICATION

In trying to make sense of the great divide that separates red states from blue states, liberal and moderate from conservatives, left from right, etc., there are two words that come to mind.

The first is wisdom.

Wisdom is gained through an accumulation of knowledge and experience. It involves the ability to discern inner qualities and relationships; to use good sense and judgment; to decide with soundness, prudence, and intelligence; to use acquired knowledge and experience to make intelligent decisions.

Wisdom is often referred to in connection with common sense, rational judgment, critical thinking, and wise words and deeds.

The second is gratification.

Regardless of whether gratification is instant or long-term, it involves receiving some form of pleasure or satisfaction. When a person indulges is a dish of ice cream, or is told something that satisfies his or her emotions and feelings, that person is gratified.

There is no downside to too much wisdom; there is a downside to too much gratification. Psychologists say an over-reliance on gratification can create problems by changing our brains, distracting us from more meaningful pursuits, and leading to destructive financial, social, and health outcomes. When the purpose is to gratify or satisfy, people naturally want to satisfy or please an audience. That audience frequently includes critics, voters, etc.

Against this backdrop, focus on voter satisfaction and listen to the language of the two major political parties.

Democrats are policy wonks. Infrastructure. Expanding health care, Social Security. Medicare. Medicaid. From workers' rights to protecting the environment; from equal pay to fighting the special interests, Democrats believe government can and should make life better for families across our nation. Government must enact those programs for all middle-class Americans and those struggling to get there.

Each of these initiatives, however, requires legislation, a process that is intense, complex and convoluted. The joke is that there are two things no one wants to see made: sausage and legislation. The exact quote comes from the 19th-century Prussian politician, Otto Von Bismarck who said, "Laws are like sausages. It is best not to see them being made." This line has been repeated millions of times since then as a good description of the legislative process. Putting it bluntly, legislation is a messy.

Each of these initiatives also involves the exercise of wisdom so that was is enacted provides the intended benefits for the affected citizens.

Republicans on the other hand frequently use convenient sound bites as substitutes for legislation. They are for less government, less taxes and more freedom from government regulation. That means whatever Democrats want to pass, Republicans are against; and whatever they manage to pass, Republicans want to repeal. It's much easier to get voters' attention to simply oppose something or to repeal a law via soundbite than it is to excite the masses over detailed policy issues.

They label anything they don't like as "tax and spend," or "socialism" or some other word or short phrase that resonates with the voters. It's much easier to oppose or condemn with a single emotive word than it is to oppose through a line-by-line analytical refutation. Analysis is not part of the Republican playbook when it comes to exciting their voters.

This is where Republicans play the gratification card. And they do it most successfully.

If the issue is gun regulation, for example, the immediate Republican response is "they're taking away our constitutional rights." Never mind that there is no constitutional right to sell, buy, or own an assault rifle; the mere raising of the "constitutional rights" red flag energizes their voters who thereby in turn become the beneficiaries of gratification when Republicans promise no such laws will be passed.

If the issue is social security, health care, generally expanding the nation's social safety net, etc., Republicans typically meet these proposals with cries of "socialism."

This of course energizes their voters because they've been conditioned to believe that anything that smacks of socialism is evil incarnate. Never mind that many of these voters are on Social Security and Medicare, or will depend on both down the road. What is important is that these voters be immediately gratified by knowing Republicans will be fighting on the front lines to prevent America from becoming socialist. Truth of course doesn't matter; it's what arouses and gratifies that counts.

If the issue is infrastructure, Republicans resort to "tax and spend," and for the party faithful, they are told infrastructure doesn't apply to their problems; it's designed to fix roads and bridges in those poor neighborhoods where folks get handouts these taxpayers/voters pay for. Again, policy is difficult; slogans and buzzwords that evoke emotion are simple and provide the intended gratification.

History informs that there have been times in America where we had less government; it was called laissez faire, which means "leave alone." It was government's attitude toward business of letting things take their own course, without interfering; government abstention from interfering in the workings of the free market. Those who ran the government believed in "laissez-faire capitalism;" that the less the government is involved in the economy, the better off business will be, and by extension, society as a whole.

History is also clear that greed is very real when people are left to their own devices. Greed is a human frailty marked by a selfish and excessive desire for more of something (such as money) than is needed. We saw this with the Robber Barons of the early 20th century, and the Roaring '20s when economic excesses led to the greatest economic collapse in American history, the Great Depression. It took those "socialist" programs along with World War II (and the battle against the prevailing Republican isolationist mood at the time) to get America back on its feet again.

And in a perverse, Machiavellian way, it makes perfect sense for Florida Gov. Ron DeSantis to wrap his restrictions, limitations, conditions, etc., in the flag of freedom. Understanding the curriculum and books he's banning; the academic freedom he's tarnishing; the businesses he's disrupting because they don't agree with him, etc., requires some level of wisdom. The "freedom" soundbite gives his audience gratification that trumps the wisdom necessary to see the forest through the trees.

What these emotive words, slogans and sound bites do is block out the wisdom necessary to formulate policies that are designed for the well-being of our growing and expanding nation, and the ability to discern the truth from the con.

Gratification, instant and prolonged, works against needed policy initiatives. It's designed to make people feel good without really knowing or caring why. They just know that when those famous words and slogans are tossed into the mix, they're gratified because Republicans have their backs. So long as the results bear fruit, this gratification strategy will continue.

It will be up to each American to know the difference between wisdom and gratification, and act appropriately for the benefit of the greater good.

ON IQ TESTS, AMERICA RANKS 29ᵀᴴ IN THE WORLD; FLORIDA RANKS 38ᵀᴴ AMONG THE STATES. IS THIS SIGNIFICANT IN MEASURING INTELLIGENCE AS IT RELATES TO POLITICAL PREFERENCES?

I came across an article today that said liberals are better educated and more intelligent than conservatives. Well, I thought, that's certainly a very general statement. Does it mean all liberals are better educated and therefore more intelligent than all conservatives? Of course not. Generalizations like this are at best misleading and at worse clearly wrong because there are always exceptions. But I thought this might be worth looking into.

There's certainly been a lot of discussion about relative intelligence level in explaining the nation's divide between red and blue states, between liberals and conservatives. To be sure, over the past decade or so, several studies have shown that people who tend to hold more conservative views score low on measures of intelligence. However, studies also show that while conservatism and intelligence are negatively correlated, the link may not be currently as strong as originally noted.

Stripped to its essence, the argument goes something like this: liberals contend that they are better educated and therefore more intelligent than conservatives; conservatives counter that this belief is driven by self-serving liberals generally and liberal scientists who conduct these studies; people who are out of touch with reality and don't understand the real interests and needs of the people. They further contend that formal education by itself is not the be-all and end-all of intelligence measurement.

The fact is, however, that the single most commonly relied upon measurement for gauging overall general intelligence is the IQ, or Intelligent Quotient, test score; and according to those companies that conduct IQ tests, the current average score for the United States is around 98.

Scientists agree that IQ is a measure of a person's reasoning ability. In other words, an IQ test is supposed to gauge how well someone can use information and logic to answer questions or make predictions. It is a measure of human intelligence. According to several studies on this subject, people who want to have their IQ measured take standardized tests and receive a score that ranks their intelligence level. The higher one's IQ score, the more intelligent that person is considered to be.

The number actually represents how one person's results compare to those of other people of the same age. A score of 116 or more is considered above average. A score of 130 or higher signals a high IQ. Membership in Mensa, the High IQ society, includes people who score in the top two percent, which is usually 132 or higher.

There is general agreement among the experts that IQ scores typically reflect the quality of education and resources available to people in their local geographic region. Areas of the world with lower IQ scores are typically poorer and less developed, particularly in the area of education, compared to countries with higher IQ scores. This understanding also applies to the several states as well.

Many researchers use IQ scores to determine the smartest countries in the world.

With that average IQ of 98 points, America ranks 29th in the world.

At this point, it's important to note that IQ isn't the only way to measure intelligence. There are actually many different ways to seek out intelligence, and many of them have nothing to do with average IQ. For instance, it's possible to analyze academic test scores. Group tests (such as the California Achievement Tests and the SAT, the Scholastic Assessment Test) are often used to measure aptitude, the capacity to learn (including both verbal and performance aptitudes) and achievement. The Wechsler (WAIS) Test is thought of by experts as an alternative to the Binet IQ test, and is the preeminent tool for testing adult intelligence levels. Also, the level of introduction of new technologies and even the number of Nobel Prize recipients—or all combined—also reveal intelligence levels.

IQ tests have long been a subject of debate in terms of measuring intelligence. The average IQ scores in America are calculated based on the scores of a standardized IQ test taken by a representative sample of the population. This data is used to determine the national average IQ score, which can be compared to the scores of other countries around the world.

Although they are widely used and accepted as a standard method for assessing cognitive ability, they have limitations. Experts and IQ critics note there are many factors that come into play when measuring intelligence, and some states may score higher on average IQ tests than others due to factors beyond their population's actual intelligence. Specifically, some studies have shown that the results of IQ tests may be influenced by culture, socioeconomic status, or other environmental factors, which can lead to inaccuracies in measuring intelligence.

Despite these limitations, IQ tests still remain one of the most commonly used methods for measuring intelligence both here and abroad.

In 2019, the top 10 countries with the highest IQ scores were: Japan - 106.49, Taiwan - 106.47, Singapore - 105.89, Hong Kong (China) - 105.37, China - 104.10, South Korea - 102.35, Belarus - 101.60, Finland - 101.20, Liechtenstein - 101.07, and Netherlands and Germany (tie) - 100.74

Here in America, the states with the highest IQ are: Massachusetts – 104.3, New Hampshire – 104.2, Vermont – 103.8, North Dakota – 103.8, Minnesota – 103.7, Montana – 103.4, Maine – 103.4, Iowa – 103.2 Connecticut – 103.1 and Wisconsin – 102.9.

From this study, northeastern and midwestern states dominate the top 10, IQs ranging from 104.3-to 102.9. At 104.3, Massachusetts has an average IQ over 10 points higher than the bottom state.

States with the lowest IQ scores are: Mississippi – 94.2, Louisiana – 95.3, California – 95.5, Hawaii – 95.6, New Mexico – 95.7, Alabama – 95.7, Nevada – 96.5, Arizona – 97.4, Arkansas – 97.5, and Tennessee – 97.7

Mississippi has the lowest average IQ at 94.2.

Florida, with an IQ score of 98.4, ranks 38th.

The numbers are what they are; nevertheless, the debate over intelligence continues as it relates to preferences for one's political philosophy.

RNC CHAIR SAYS PRESIDENTIAL CANDIDATES MUST SIGN A LOYALTY PLEDGE TO TAKE PART IN 2024 DEBATES. DREAM ON

Here's one that is more hope than reality. Does the RNC chair really believe Donald Trump will agree to support the party's nominee next year if it's not him? Does she really believe she can tell the 800-pound gorilla and former president in that room that he can't get on the stage to debate the other candidates? Noting his penchant for dishonesty, does she really believe Trump would keep such a pledge even if he signed it? Does she really believe Trump's supercharged ego will accept being upstaged by someone else (translation: Ron DeSantis) being nominated?

If Trump perceives his nomination is a lost cause, he'll do what he did in Georgia: tell the voters the system is rigged and they should stay home. Or he'll take his tens of millions of votes and try to form a third party (although timing would be a problem).

If he's not the nominee, he would rather diss his party's chances and see a Democrat win. This would allow him the convenience of criticizing a Democratic president from afar without being unfavorably compared to a Republican presidential successor.

I think the Republican leadership would love to thank Trump for his service and move on beyond him, but he remains a force; the party leaders don't want to have Trump's base jump ship or sit out 2024. The alienation issue remains a potent consideration.

While there are circumstances that could take Trump out of the picture completely and make him a non-issue, remaining in the party's mix with all his baggage certainly doesn't hurt the Democrats.

George Waas

THE REPUBLICAN PARTY IS THE PARTY OF LAW AND ORDER? THINK AGAIN

Whenever there's a protest in the name of police brutality, abortion, academic freedom, censorship, voting rights—indeed, any subject identified with liberalism or progressivism--you can bet the Republican Party leaders will raise a hue and cry. They loudly remind the masses that they are the party of law and order, wrapping themselves in the American Flag, champions of freedom, standing on the side of law enforcement everywhere against those evildoers and anarchists.

They expect their supporters to nod their heads in agreement, and treat the protestors as anti-government socialists who are against our proud defenders of freedom, liberty and justice.

All that is necessary, however, to see the forest through the trees on this is to give their flag-waving and chest-beating some thought.

What exactly does law and order mean to Republicans? Judging from their conduct over the past few years, law and order applies only to left wing demonstrations and protests.

Let's look at two glaring examples.

First, the January 6 attack on the nation's capital was carried out by right wing extremists egged on by a Republican president and several Republican members of Congress.

294

Five died in that attack, including law enforcement officers. Several more officers died by suicide stemming from that insurrection.

This was a Republican-led assault on our nation's greatest symbol of Democracy, and an assault on law enforcement officers sworn to uphold the Constitution and laws of the land.

Where was the party's loud and vigorous support for law and order on that fateful day?

Where was the party's outrage that lives were lost and precious property damaged all in the name of giving vent to a lie forged by a sitting Republican president against the completion of the constitutionally mandated peaceful transfer of power?

This tragic event was the first time in our nation's history that the peaceful transfer of power was violated. Rather than acting to assure that such a horrific display of totalitarianism is never repeated, Republicans doubled down. First, party leaders said Donald Trump committed no crime; then the party's national committee outrageously said January 6 was nothing more than loyal supporters engaging in legitimate public discourse.

Rather than condemning in no uncertain terms this violence against law and order in the form of police officers defending the capital and the constitutional process, Republicans attempted to gaslight the entire tragedy, hoping the public would deny what they saw and heard with their own senses.

Recall the videos of officers being beaten with the American flag, sprayed with a pungent chemical; uniformed officers fighting for their lives against a right-wing mob. Republicans tried to gaslight this by first saying it was Antifa, fecklessly trying to place blame on those "liberal leftist socialist communists." When people of reason saw through that nonsense, the party reacted with its typical silence, then tried to deflect by scapegoating the entire tragedy in the form of a promised investigation of Hunter Biden and the Biden family.

Hundreds of members of Congress bought into that lie. Today, we still have among us election deniers who would presumably repeat their actions—particularly their support for what transpired on January 6—in the name of protecting their criminal-in-chief.

Republicans should well understand that they can't legitimately claim the high road on law and order while giving lip service to what those extremists did on January 6. They can't truly be for law and order if they remain silent while their ex-president even considers handing out pardons to the lawbreakers who attacked law enforcement officers, among others.

Has House Speaker Kevin McCarthy or Senate Minority Leader Mitch McConnell and their backers ever uttered a word of condemnation for this conduct? Not a word.

How about their defense of their liar-in-chief over his illegal call to the Ukraine president seeking dirt on Hunter Biden in return for release of approved funds? The law is clear that such a quid pro quo by a president is against the nation's laws. Where was their stand on law and order then?

And about those stolen government records. Where is the Republican party's cry of law and order when a departing president takes records that by law are to go to the National Archives for preservation, houses them in his residence, strews them around his property, and falsely says he turned over all records when he still knowingly possessed some?

Again, rather than condemning this illegal behavior, congressional Republicans doubled down, vowing to take on the FBI for discharging its legal duties by holding accountable a scofflaw president who believes the law doesn't apply to him, or he can decide what the law is.

Law and order? Hardly.

For my second example, we need only to look at what Gov. Ron DeSantis is doing in Florida. This wannabee president is a well-educated man. He knows that the First Amendment to the United States Constitution provides in significant part that:

"Congress shall make no law ...abridging the freedom of speech ...or the right of the people peaceably to assemble, and to petition the Government for a redress of grievances."

But DeSantis and his minions will have none of it. These Florida Republicans are doing everything they can to place peaceful protests far enough away from the halls of government so they won't hear or see what the protestors are demonstrating about.

The value of any peaceful protest is directly related to the ability of the officials who are the subject of the protest to learn of citizens' concerns, and act accordingly. Silencing protestors by distance does violence to the confluence of constitutional rights that allows for that protest in the first place.

They firmly believe that out of sight is out of mind so they can pass whatever laws they want with impunity, because they don't believe anyone can stop them. As for reliance on the courts, DeSantis and his willing accomplices have done their part to forge a compliant judiciary. And even if they should lose in court, the protest would have been barred by that time anyway. If damages have to be paid for the loss of the exercise of a constitutional right, the taxpayers will foot the bill. How convenient!

The right to protest is a manifestation of the right to freedom of assembly, the right to freedom of association, and the right to freedom of speech all protected and guaranteed by our Constitution. But in Florida, these rights don't apply to those who want to protest against draconian Republican plans to strip academic freedom, control what is taught in schools, control what can be said in schools, and punish anyone who dares to question or complain about them.

And now DeSantis wants to make Florida the model for America by taking his act to Washington D.C. What a model!

The next time Republicans wrap the law and order flag around themselves, think (a dangerous thing for them) about how they treat law and order when it's aimed at their actions. Listen to what they say, but more importantly, watch what they do.

WHAT IS YOUR STORY WORTH?

The more precise question is what is your life story worth?

A little over ten years ago, I had major orthopedic surgery that required more than a year of recovery time. I had just retired and wondered how I would get through this lengthy recovery downtime.

Over the years, I related stories about my childhood and early adult life to my wife and children, and was encouraged by them to put my stories on paper. I hesitated, until something else entered the picture: although Ancestry. com had been around since 1983, the beginning of DNA testing in 2012 led to an explosion of interest in uncovering family history. This discovery played into peoples' innate desire to know where they come from and who they are though their ancestors. I also realized that, unfortunately, vital statistical records going back a few generations were not well kept. They were handwritten (often illegibly) and, in many cases, destroyed by fire or flood. (Fortunately, Records going forward are well-kept today.)

All of these thoughts convinced me that that was the proper time to write a lengthy memoir that was published in 2012.

When I decided to go forward with my plan in 2012, I wrote out in longhand an outline, a chronological listing of events and occurrences that I could recall. Needless to say, recalling important events over almost 70 years was a daunting experience. As I began the actual process of writing, I was amazed at how quickly the words appeared on my computer screen. It was as if the memoir was writing itself, passing from my mind through my fingers onto the page.

I promised my family and I kept my promise.

Being pleased at what I accomplished, two years later, while taking a memoir writing class at Florida State University, I wrote a shorter, and in my view, better version than my stream-of-conscience effort of two years earlier.

Which brings me to the heart of my message to you.

It isn't necessary any longer to draft an outline and write a memoir on a computer screen to tell your life story.

There is one company that makes it easy to tell your life's story. There may well be others.

More on that shortly.

Why tell your story?

The growing emphasis on ancestry tells me that people are interested in, and fascinated with, our past. We want to know about our lineage; who our great-grandparents were; who their parents were; as far back as records can take us. But for generations going forward, it's important for our children, our children's children, and on and on, that they know about their great-grandparents, grandparents, parents, etc. That's where telling your story comes in.

What better way is there to leave a legacy for your children and their children—generation after generation—than writing your life story? The only way they will truly know who you are is if you tell them in your own words in a format that will be a permanent family legacy. No filter, no interpretive gloss. Your strengths and weaknesses, trials and tribulations, warts and all. Writing your story allows you to open up, be honest and revealing. Future generations that will never meet you will nevertheless get to know you.

No one knows your life story better than you, so why not write it? Each person has led a life different from everyone else. Each person has had unique experiences; no two people have led identical lives. Share your uniqueness with your family. There is no downside to that.

And the best part is now there is an easy way to tell your story.

I found out about Storyworth when my daughters, unbeknownst to me, set up an online account whereby each week for 52 weeks I receive a question via email that I must respond to as best as I can. Each Monday since last July, I receive a question that I answer in narrative form via a return email. That's all there is to it.

Storyworth is a subscription service that collects those answers, which are favorite stories and memories, and preserves them in a bound book. The subscription lasts for a year, but this company gives storytellers a three-month grace period to allow time to add, edit, and review their stories before finalizing their book, though there are no hard limits on when this can be done.

For the 52 questions, subscribers can choose their questions from the company's library, edit those questions, or even write their own, so they have full flexibility with the topics the storyteller can write about.

These 52 questions are designed to elicit one's life story. Here are a few examples of the questions I get each week:

What memories do you have of your father (his name, birth date, birthplace, parents, and so on)?

What memories do you have of your mother (her name, birth date, birthplace, parents, and so on)?

What kind of work did your parents do (farmer, salesman, manager, seamstress, nurse, stay-at-home mom, professional, laborer, and so on)?

What kind of hardships or tragedies did your family experience while you were growing up?

What are the names of your siblings? Describe things that stand out in your mind about each of your siblings.

What were some of your family traditions?

Share some memories of your grandparents.

Who were your aunts and uncles? Write about any of your aunts or uncles who really stand out in your mind. Give some details about them (names, personalities, events that you remember doing with them, and so on).

Where did you go to school? Provide some details about what was school like for you and some of your memorable experiences.

What were your favorite subjects in school? Explain why.

What subjects did you like the least? Explain why.

Each book has a maximum page count of 480 pages. If the 52 narrative responses stories exceed this page limitation, they can be split up into separate volumes for an additional cost. The subscription cost is $99 and includes the finished hardcover book once the story-writing is complete. Additional books can be purchased for as low as $39.

The subscribers, in this case my daughters, always have full control over who can see my stories. All stories are private by default, and only shared with family members I invite to read them. No stories are published publicly.

It was that very first question last July that told me what my daughters wanted to do for my 80th birthday this July.

It couldn't be easier to share your life story now. All it takes is a few minutes one day each week for a year, and your family will have a precious gift from you.

WHO IS REALLY ENGAGING IN "CANCEL CULTURE?"

Republicans have successfully weaponized "woke" by perverting its meaning. The dictionary definition of woke means "aware of and actively attentive to important societal facts and issues (especially issues of racial and social justice). " This hasn't stopped Republicans from converting "woke" into an epithet against liberals to the point where it means something distasteful or evil—largely by convincing their loyal, unthinking supporters that being anti-woke, or ignorant, is a good thing.

But they didn't stop with "woke." The right wing also co-opted "cancel culture" to mean whatever evil the liberals and moderates are doing to "damage" the "conservative viewpoint."

"Cancel culture" is defined as "a phenomenon in which those who are deemed to have acted or spoken in an unacceptable manner are ostracized, boycotted or shunned." I suppose this means that condemning racist rants subjects the critics to the charge of engaging in cancel culture. Good for them.

During the most recent midterm elections, Republicans piled it on Democrats by accusing them of engaging in "cancel culture" tactics. Just about every time a conservative uttered a ridiculous or off-the-wall comment, or behaved in a ludicrous or juvenile manner, and was criticized by the Democrats, Republicans dipped into their bag of buzzwords and accused the Democrats of engaging in "cancel culture." Republicans made "I won't be cancelled" a hue and cry addition to their supply of verbal weapons of outrage.

Republicans have mastered buzzwords that turn voters on and out by appealing to their fears, anger, resentment and hatred. For the party faithful, the historic buzzwords, such as the bland "tax and spend," doesn't inflame and arouse passions like the images conjured up by accusations of "cancel culture."

As one author put it, this buzz phrase "captures the lurking intuition haunting many voters that they are slowly disappearing from the American mainstream; pushed to the margins of American life and culture, they suspect, by new forces ranging from inexorable demographic change to insistent political correctness. It doesn't matter whether you and I agree with their assessments; they vote the way they feel, and the term "cancel culture" toxically distills their feelings." Again, it's all about instilling anger and resentment. Facts mustn't get in the way.

But here's the irony. Whatever the "woke" left has done to justify the recent cancel culture attack, the extreme right has weaponized it for years. If you want examples of "cancel culture," look no further than Florida, which has provided the lead to other red states in restricting voting rights; trampling academic freedom; restricting free speech; banning books; suppressing legitimate peaceful protest; punishing those who dare to question their authoritarian rule; and canceling or censoring what we read, think and say—all in the name of freedom. It doesn't get more "cancel culture" than that.

There is no more profound and tragic a display of cancel culture than right wing extremists invading our nation's capital in a violent attempt to cancel the constitutional counting of electoral college votes in the 2020 presidential election. Collateral examples of cancel culture are those Republican officials who even now seek to render illegitimate Joe Biden's presidency and the more than 81 million who voted for him by persisting in election denial. That they continually and brazenly lie is the height of cancel culture.

Other examples of Republican engagement in cancel culture abound. But, sadly, party officials will ignore them while plowing their loyal supporters with drivel to keep them angry, resentful, but above all, deeply enraged and engaged. In short, the party will feed them garbage, and the base will eat it up.

That's cancel culture.

FOX NEWS REPEATED THE "BIG LIE" TO PROTECT ITS BRAND AND PRESERVE THE CONSERVATIVE POINT OF VIEW. DEPLORABLE

We now learn that the head of Fox corporation, Rupert Murdoch, as well as his corporate underlings, knew that the network's news entertainers Sean Hannity, Tucker Carlson and others were lying on air night after night, filling their viewers with Donald Trump's Big Lie of a rigged election.

They fanned the flames of anger for one central purpose: to save the Fox brand. The network gurus feared their audience would shift to other, even more extreme, right wing media, so they lied and lied and lied ad infinitum ad nauseam.

What is that brand today? Millions will say "Well, what did you expect? Fox News has been a shill for the extreme right wing of the Republican Party for years. Any semblance of a journalism medium with integrity and honesty has now been thoroughly exposed, but we knew it all along. Nothing new here."

Sadly, however, millions will also say "Oh, there's nothing wrong here. It's just another example of liberal fake news. So what if Fox News might have engaged in a bit of embellishment. One of our new political stars, George Santos, embellished a bit, and that's perfectly fine and necessary to promote the conservative point of view."

Embellishment? Conservative point of view?

Is lying to this extreme representative of the conservative point of view? Donald Trump made lying, as well as cheating and stealing, acceptable. He says he "did nothing wrong" and his loyalists either nod their head in agreement or remain curiously silent. Are cheating and stealing also part of the conservative point of view?

In ordinary times, the kind of revelations about an organization that passes itself off as a major news network would be roundly embarrassing, forcing its operatives to hang their heads in shame, seeking forgiveness and promising to never betray the public trust again.

But these aren't ordinary times. Fox may lose some money in a major lawsuit that has unearthed these revelations, but it will not suffer any decline in viewership. The audience supports extreme politicians and their media shills in believing that the end--ridiculing and stamping out Democrats and anyone else who has the audacity to challenge or question the party's extremists--justifies whatever means are taken by party leaders and their network lemmings.

Fox News has as one of its slogans "Fair and Balanced." This sorry episode makes a mockery of that. Calling its repeated pressing of Trump's Big Lie fair would be laughable were it not such a serious breach of the public trust. Perhaps it's a reflection of how Fox really views its audience. Do the Fox folks believe their audience is just a bunch of angry people who will gleefully accept the dung dished out night after night? If so, what a low opinion Fox has of its audience.

Fox also has another slogan "America is Watching." We now know what America is seeing. For millions, a Lying News Network. A False News Network. But for millions more, it's just a shrug of the shoulders and a reminder that this is what is necessary to protect the conservative point of view.

There is another word that accurately describes this entire sorry scenario: Deplorable.

AFTER PUTTING DISNEY IN ITS PLACE, GOV. RON DESANTIS TAKES AIM AT THE PRESS BY PROPOSING A CHANGE TO DEFAMATION LAW

Fresh from his victory over Disney, punishing Florida's significant employer for questioning Ron DeSantis' "Don't Say Gay" stand, the presidential aspirant now has in his line of sight defamation and libel law. The United States Supreme Court opined in 1964 that in order for a public official to successfully sue for defamation, a victim has to prove "actual malice", meaning that no public official could win damages for libel without proving that the statement was made "with knowledge that it was false or with reckless disregard of whether it was false or not." Reckless disregard means the publisher had a high degree of awareness of probable falsity, or that he in fact entertained serious doubts as to the statement's truth.

This high standard, however, is too much for DeSantis. He wants to make it easier to sue the media for making false statements. DeSantis wants this; his deferential legislators want this; therefore, it will pass in some form or another.

The thrust of this bill is to accomplish what occurred with abortion--removing federal constitutional protection and sending the issue back to the states. In short, supporters of this bill want to have each state decide for itself what constitutes defamation. The difference between the abortion issue and this one is that the word "abortion" doesn't appear anywhere in the Constitution; while the First Amendment clearly protects free speech and free press nationwide. But that issue is for another day.

If this bill becomes law, it will be fought tooth and nail in the courts, all the way to the Supreme Court.

If DeSantis' bill becomes law, it would make it easier to sue the news media for publishing false statements. Presumably, it would also make it easier to sue public officials for making false statements.

Like Fox News and Ron DeSantis, for example.

Be careful what you wish for.

"DON'T WORRY BE HAPPY"

The other day, I heard this song on the radio. It's an oldie but goodie, from 1988. The theme is obvious, as this one line shows: "in your life expect some trouble but when you worry, you make it double..." It occurred to me this song captures the essence of the nation's current political climate: the drive by conservatives to eliminate worry and make us happy.

Conservatives are clear about wanting to take America back to a "better time": a time of Reconstruction, the Gilded Age, the Roaring '20s. Back when American was largely unregulated; when businesses flourished, when the government's approach was generally "out of sight, out of mind;" when "the business of America (was) business" as President Calvin Coolidge is reputed to have said.

Back then, the conservative view was that if business was successful, employees wouldn't worry; families wouldn't worry; no one would worry; and everybody would be happy.

It's that state of happiness; sublime blissfulness, that conservatives want for all Americans.

Standing in the way of this plan for total contentment, however, are obstacles such as our nation's history--the truth about our past; and anything that depicts our nation and our people in a negative light.

Recall the lyrics from the theme song of "All in the Family," a comedy series that ran on CBS beginning more than 50 years ago. The song is entitled "Those Were The Days" and those titled words were repeated throughout. Here are the main lyrics:

Guys like me we had it made

Didn't need no welfare state
ev'rybody pulled his weight

And you knew who you were then
girls were girls and men were men
Mister we could use a man like Herbert Hoover again

People seemed to be content
fifty dollars paid the rent
freaks were in a circus tent

Take a little Sunday spin
go to watch the Dodgers win

Hair was short and skirts were long
I don't know just what went wrong

See anything familiar here? Those were the days when people knew their place. They looked the same; those who were different were sidelined. They took their minds off their woes by going for a drive or a baseball game. People were content. This theme song is 50 years old; it could have been written yesterday.

Conservatives hold to a belief today that everything would have been fine after the stock market Crash of 1929 had Herbert Hoover been re-elected. Conservatives maintain that Hoover was correct when he said "prosperity was just around the corner" even as the nation's economy crashed and burned. Still, conservatives believe America wouldn't have had to turn to "socialism" and "liberalism" when "traditional market forces" would have worked. Instead, they believe America foolishly opted for a philosophy of government handouts and giveaways to people who didn't earn them, paid by those who worked and had their tax dollars given to the shiftless and lazy. Missing from this is any recognition of unregulated businesses running wild, speculating mightily, devaluing the dollar and sending the nation's economy over the cliff.

Conservatives make no bones about it; they oppose all social service and economic safety net programs unless they are of significant benefit to the corporate and business world.

If they have their druthers, they will most assuredly revamp Social Security, Medicare, Medicaid, and all programs they believe are giveaways, even those imagined. The will take a cleaver to them, either drastically cutting or eliminating them.

But they won't be content with that.

Lurking in the background of their collective mindset is their ultimate plan: the creation of a society of happiness as they define it. Conservatives are hellbent on removing all things that undercut this plan.

They believe the ultimate key to happiness is elimination of worry. The phrase "ignorance is bliss" is most appropriate because it means if you do not know about something, you do not worry about it.

Conservatives are going all-out to remove all things that cause psychological distress. They are cutting curriculum that teaches inconvenient truths about us. They are banning books so no one will read things that cause distress or worry. They are eliminating programs of advanced study to dumb down the best and brightest so they won't have the skills to ask pesky questions. They are punishing those who step out of line and thereby cause distress and worry. Conservatives believe anyone who questions their actions are interfering with the public's happiness, and those who interfere are enemies of the people. And they have tens of millions of loyalists cheering them on. They long for the day when they don't have to worry anymore; when they will be happy when their leaders tell them they are.

Conservatives know what's best for everyone and can't have anyone or anything interfere with their happiness plans.

Those who see through the conservatives' forest ask: What about facts? Facts, for conservatives, are only those that lead to happiness. Other so-called facts are harmful and must be eliminated.

Inquiring minds further ask: What about the truth? Conservatives say the only real truth lies in the values that make America great; like the words of the Declaration of Independence. A natural follow-up question is: But does our nation's history bear up to those words? Conservatives deflect on this one, countering instead that their plans will match those words to actual conduct.

Conservatives will cleanse worry from everyone's minds by reworking our nation's education systems to eliminate negativity; removing books that give off negative feelings; cut programs that help students to learn to think logically and critically because these programs cause worry; re-define academic freedom consistent with good feelings and contentment; and do whatever else is necessary to remove all putative obstacles and convince the public that they are happy.

And as for truth, remember that movie line "You can't handle the truth?" Conservatives say everyone can handle the truth, providing truth is properly defined so that it corresponds with their goal of national happiness.

But thinking minds ask: won't this lead to a dumbed down nation; a nation of ignorant, stupid people incapable of keeping up with the rest of the world?

Don't worry.

Be happy.

Printed in the United States
by Baker & Taylor Publisher Services